ARCTIC OCEAN

◆RUSSIA

NORTH

PACIFIC

OCEAN

TURKEY

INDIAN

OCEAN

MARQUESAS
ISLANDS ●

The World
of
DAVID GLASGOW FARRAGUT

● **Important Places in Farragut's Life**
◆ **Countries Visited During the Admiral's Yearlong European Tour**

FULL SPEED AHEAD!

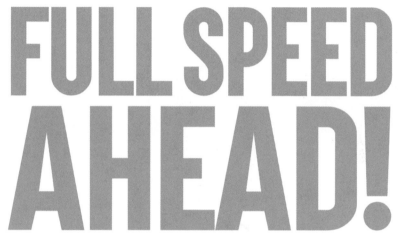

FULL SPEED AHEAD!

AMERICA'S FIRST ADMIRAL: DAVID GLASGOW FARRAGUT

LOUISE BORDEN

CALKINS CREEK
AN IMPRINT OF BOYDS MILLS & KANE
New York

For information about permission to reproduce selections from this book,
please contact permissions@bmkbooks.com.

Calkins Creek
An imprint of Boyds Mills & Kane, a division of Astra Publishing House
calkinscreekbooks.com
Printed in China

ISBN: 978-1-68437-905-7 (hc)
ISBN: 978-1-63592-464-0 (eBook)
Library of Congress Control Number: 2020947746

First edition
10 9 8 7 6 5 4 3 2 1

Design by Red Herring Design
The text is set in Kepler Light.
The titles are set in Aku & Kamu and Brothers.

To Pete, Cindy, and Alex . . .
our blue lake sailors

and

to Carolyn Yoder . . .
my exceptional editor and navigator

"I have been devoted to the service of my country since I was eight years of age."

—DAVID GLASGOW FARRAGUT

*December 12, 1864,
in a speech in New York City*

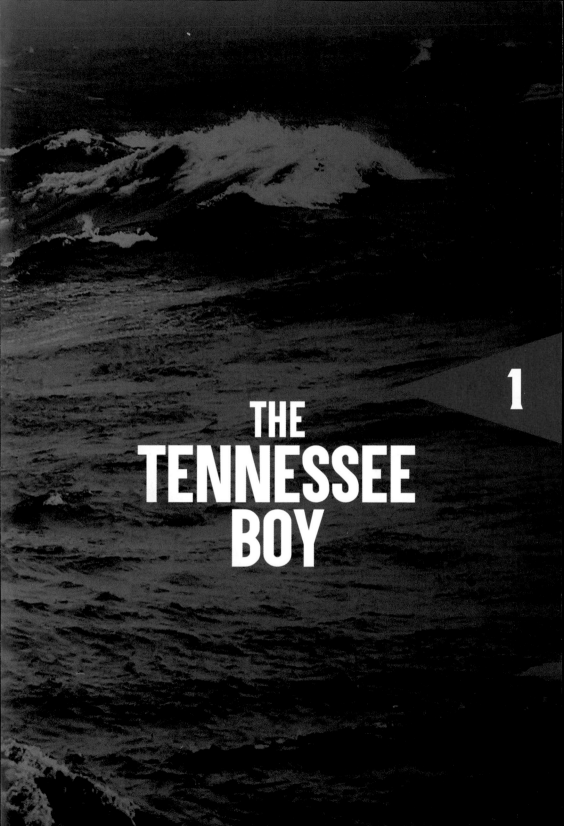

THE TENNESSEE BOY

1

This portrait of George Farragut (painted some years after his death in 1817) is attributed to American painter William Swain (1803–1847).

WINTER 1806–1807

At Stony Point on the Holston,
James Glasgow Farragut . . . called Glasgow,
had never seen an ocean.

But at age five,
he knew the river
that glittered in the Tennessee sunshine.

And the distant hills
of the Cumberland Mountains.

And the log cabin, built by his father . . .
with gun slots in the walls
and a bar and chain on the door
to keep the family safe
on their six hundred and forty acres.

And he knew the ferry
George Farragut poled from the north side
of the Holston
to the south side and back again . . .
carrying travelers
who brought news from the village of Knoxville,
fifteen miles away.

To Glasgow and his brother William,
who was nine,
their stocky papa was a man of *action* . . .

on his ferry
where he greeted all as friends
or on this frontier,
where he'd gallop off on his horse
to help neighbors
in his uniform with gold epaulets.

Major Farragut in the state militia.

Their mother Elizabeth
was like a bright sun in the dim cabin.

She could sew a shirt,
write with a quill pen,
say prayers to God,
teach those prayers to her children,
or help run the ferry
when the Holston was wrapped in mist.

On cold nights
after Nancy, who turned three in January,
was tucked in bed
and their brother George was in his cradle,
Glasgow and William heard tales
of Elizabeth who grew up in North Carolina
before it was a state . . .
and of her family, named Shine,
who ran a ferry on the French Broad River.

And they heard of Ciutadella

Ciutadella!

on the sunny island of Minorca,
near Spain ...
where their father George had been born
and named *Jordi Ferragut Mesquida*.

Jordi ...
who went to school in Barcelona
and sailed the Mediterranean
as a boy on *his* father's ship ...
who left Minorca at eighteen to cross the Atlantic Ocean ...

who traded out of New Orleans
and in 1776,
smuggled cannon below deck
past the British to patriots in Charleston ...

who changed his name to *George Farragut*
when he joined South Carolina's navy
in the war for independence ...
and who led soldiers on horseback
against the enemy redcoats.

Glasgow listened to each word
as pictures swirled in his mind.

Foreign ports ... white sails ... ocean.

Someday ...

This watercolor and gouache painting is attributed to Michele Felice Corné, around 1803. It is the earliest known painting of the USS *Constitution*. Launched in 1797, the *Constitution* is the oldest commissioned ship in the US Navy. Known as "Old Ironsides," it can be visited at the Charlestown Navy Yard, Boston.

SPRING AND SUMMER 1807

Glasgow's papa had ships—
not the woods of Tennessee—
in his heart.

With his Spanish and English
and a smattering of French,
he was given a *commission*, a job as an *officer*,
in the US Navy . . .
a young navy, created in 1775
by the Continental Congress in Philadelphia
to fight the British on the sea . . .

a navy that grew
under President George Washington in 1794 . . .
with stations in American ports
and a fleet of ships to protect the coasts
with frigates, schooners, and gunboats . . .
a navy that grew even more
under President John Adams
so it could fight pirates on the seas
and protect trade . . .

a navy whose ships had fought well
against French ships
during battles in the Caribbean
called the Quasi War . . . or Almost War.

In the Quasi War, the USS *Constellation* (left) captured the French frigate *L'Insurgente* (right) on February 9, 1799. Battles were fought in the West Indies between the navies and privateer vessels of France and the US after the French seized merchant ships when the United States refused to pay some debts after the American Revolution. This painting was created by retired Rear Admiral John William Schmidt in 1981.

Now Thomas Jefferson . . .
America's third president
and the second to live in the new capital,
the city of Washington,
was the commander-in-chief . . .
and *he* signed George Farragut's commission.

That March,
the Department of the Navy
sent Glasgow's father a *warrant* . . . an oath on paper
to serve and defend his country . . .
and assigned him to the new naval station
in New Orleans, a port he already knew.

On April 1,
George returned the warrant
with a note that he was working on a craft
to transport his wife and children
to New Orleans.

That craft was a flatboat . . .
and Glasgow and William helped carry tools and logs
to the bank of the Holston
as the deck and cabin took shape.

Before the flatboat was finished,
their papa packed his saddlebags
and headed by horseback
and then by river . . .

to report for duty.

On July 1 in New Orleans,
the name *George Farragut* was added to the *muster roll* . . .
the list of those serving at the naval station.
And four days later, at Stony Point,
Glasgow had his sixth birthday . . .
with his sailor papa miles away.

Over the next weeks,
Merrill Brady, a family friend from Kentucky,
notched the last planks on the flatboat
while Glasgow,
and William who turned ten in August,
helped Elizabeth pack barrels of food . . .
and all they owned.

Then one September morning,
Glasgow's family went aboard.
Standing at the *stern*, the back,
and pulling on a long oar,
Merrill Brady moved the craft into the Holston's current,
headed downstream.

Glasgow Farragut,
the boy who dreamed of ships and the ocean,
stood on the deck, a breeze in his face.

He looked ahead . . . to his first journey on water.

FALL 1807

The Farragut boat floated down the Holston
and passed the eddies of the Tennessee and the Clinch.
Now the three rivers flowed as one . . .
the Tennessee.
Glasgow marveled at the web of watery roads
that would take him to his father and a *real* city.

With William,
he used his eyes to scout for sandbars or rocks.
Or fished from the boat.
Or helped Elizabeth care for Nancy and little George.

On each bank,
forests were alive with birds and animals . . .
and as the trees yellowed into October,
the current swept the flatboat
along the blue-gray path of the Tennessee
until Brady, at the stern,
turned the front of the craft, the *bow*,
west into the Ohio River.

O-h-i-o.

Another road of water.

Soon Merrill Brady pulled in at Fort Massac . . .
a lone outpost on the north bank
where President Jefferson's explorers, Lewis and Clark,
had made a stop four years earlier . . .
on their way to map new American lands,
purchased from France.

After buying supplies,
the Farragut family said goodbye
to soldiers and settlers
and the flatboat floated on downstream
until fifty miles later,
the Ohio met the great Mississippi . . .

Glasgow's *fourth* river.

Drifting Downriver—Flatboats on the Cumberland, painted by American artist
David Wright in 2012, shows what Tennessee flatboats that traveled on America's
rivers during the early 1800s looked like.

As the miles faded behind them,
Glasgow and William saw Cherokee
or Choctaw hunters
glide past in their canoes.
And traders with their cargoes,
headed downstream.

On and on,
the flatboat floated for almost seventeen hundred miles . . .
through territories that weren't yet states.
If Glasgow looked to his left, he saw Mississippi.
On his right was Louisiana,
and then downriver, Orleans.
For eight weeks,
this was his world on water.

Then . . .
Glasgow counted more craft on the wide river
and after Brady steered past the town of Baton Rouge,
called *red stick* by the French . . .
the flatboat came to a crescent bend.

Glasgow stood near the bow with William,
scanning the shore to his left.

New Orleans!

Their papa's city . . .
with docks and piers and ships.
A *real* city with a grid of streets and canals . . .
sailors from foreign ports . . .
rich merchants . . .
ladies in fancy hats . . .
thieves . . . and pirates.

A city with a swirl of French,
Spanish, English,
and African voices . . .
an *old* city France had won back
from the king of Spain in 1800
and then *sold* to President Jefferson in 1803.

New Orleans,
with almost ten thousand citizens
and its Lakes Pontchartrain and Borgne,
was now an American port . . .
and the Stars and Stripes fluttered
above *Place d'Armes*, the main square.

For the Tennessee boy,
everything was exotic . . .
even the soft air.

But his father George,
whom Glasgow hadn't seen in five months,
was the same stocky papa with his smile . . .
and his family was *together* again.

EVERY **THING** **PROSPERS**

This view of New Orleans, looking upriver, was painted in 1803 by J. L. Bouquet de Woiseri, artist and mapmaker, to celebrate the Louisiana Purchase by President Thomas Jefferson.

WINTER 1807–1808

In their new home,
Elizabeth tended her youngest children
and a baby also named Elizabeth,
born after the river trip,
while George took Glasgow and William
to the naval station.

There men were at work with *boats*:
sewing canvas sails . . .
replacing masts splintered by storms . . .
caulking the *hulls*,
the bottoms and sides of ships, with hot tar . . .
or training as sailors or gunners.

Glasgow's father wore a uniform
and aboard *Gunboat 11*, a schooner with two masts,
his rank was sailing master . . .
the officer who served under the captain as navigator . . .
charting where the gunboat would patrol
on the waters near New Orleans.

Sailing master!

Glasgow felt a sweep of pride
as he stood on the deck
and saw the ship's flag turn in the breeze.

The United States of America.

In the distance,
he heard the crisp roll of drums
and the shrill whistle giving orders to a crew
by the pipe of a *boatswain*,
or *bosun* . . . an officer on deck.

To young Glasgow,
the US Navy was a beacon for adventure.

A sketch showing schooners used as gunboats in the US Navy

WINTER 1807–1808

Soon Glasgow was on Lake Pontchartrain
with his father and William,
paddling in their *pirogue*,
a canoe made of two pieces of wood . . .
or sailing aboard George's *yawl*,
a boat with a main mast and a *mizzen* . . .
the mast that was *aft*
or *behind* the taller main mast.

Mizzen!

The lake was shallow
with a salty mix of ocean and river.
And forty miles long . . . *huge* to a six-year-old boy.

On Pontchartrain,
Glasgow could *see* what a tide was.

A *low tide* pulled water away from the land . . . an *ebb*.
A *high tide* pushed the sea back to it . . . a *flow*, or *flood*.

The moon and the turn of the earth and the wind
made the water rise and fall
every hour of the day and night . . .
as the tides came in and went out.

Glasgow listened to his father's lessons
in navigation
and kept each nautical word in his heart.

Port was for left . . . *starboard* for right.

Meridian was noon. *M-e-r-i-d-i-a-n.*

Squall was a sudden storm.

A *fathom* was six feet of depth.

And *masts* had sails to catch the wind
and move a ship in any direction.

North. South. East. West.

The songs of sailing.

When his sons were aboard,
Glasgow's teacher was a careful seaman.
If a squall blew whitecaps . . . waves with crests,
across the lake,
George Farragut turned his yawl
toward the shelter of an island.

"When the weather was bad
we usually slept on the beach of one of the . . . islands
in the Lake . . . wrapped in the boat sail,
and, if the weather was cold,
we . . . half buried ourselves in the dry sand,"
Glasgow wrote later in his life.

He wanted to be as fearless as his papa from Minorca . . .
steady at the helm,
trusting his own courage.

SPRING 1808

Then, in March,
Glasgow was parted from his closest friend
when *W. A. C. Farragut*
was added to the New Orleans muster roll
and William moved to the naval station.

Still ten,
he would train to be an officer
as an acting midshipman . . .
until he was sent a warrant to be a regular midshipman.

Midshipman!

A *midshipman* passed orders
from the captain and the officers to the crew.

A *midshipman* was the one in charge of his ship's small boats
when in port.

A *midshipman* studied navigation
and wrote in a journal each day.

The word dazzled Glasgow.
So did his brother's blue jacket and hat with trim.

His own uniform and warrant
were what Glasgow Farragut now dreamed about.

Someday . . .

someday . . .

SUMMER 1808

Soon the June heat seeped into the bayous . . .
the marshy outlets
of the lakes and the Mississippi . . .
and smothered New Orleans.
One afternoon,
Glasgow's father was fishing on Pontchartrain
and spotted a boat adrift . . .
with old David Porter, also a sailing master,
passed out from sunstroke.

George brought his friend home,
so Elizabeth could be his nurse.
She became ill, too . . . with yellow fever,
a virus spread by mosquitoes.

When George took his children to stay with friends,
Glasgow . . . whose mother was his sunlight on land,
never knew she was dying.

Days after her burial in late June,
George told Glasgow
that Elizabeth Farragut and David Porter
had died on the same date.

His beloved mama . . . was in heaven.

On July 5,
Glasgow had a quiet seventh birthday . . .
this year, and forever, without his mother.
With William in the navy,
he was the oldest child at home.
Nancy and little George counted on him.
And baby Elizabeth,
who cooed and smiled,
needed his love.

But still,
the Farragut family was in a fog of loss.
Their compass, Elizabeth, was gone.

FALL 1808

The *son* of Sailing Master Porter,
who'd been buried the same day in the Protestant cemetery
as Glasgow's mother,
was also named David Porter . . .
and he, too, was in the US Navy.

A midshipman at age eighteen,
then a lieutenant
who had fought the French in the Quasi War . . .
and Barbary pirates in the Mediterranean . . .
Porter was now twenty-eight,
with the rank of *commander*.
Days before his father died,
he arrived in New Orleans with his new wife, Evelina,
with orders to command the small naval station.

That September, in his own sadness,
David Porter assigned another sailing master to *Gunboat 11*,
and gave George Farragut tasks at the naval station.
Porter hoped somehow . . . someday . . .
to repay the grieving family for the care of his father.

With four children to feed,
George Farragut, age fifty-three, retired from the navy
and bought a farm on the Pascagoula River,
a hundred miles east of New Orleans,
near the Gulf of Mexico . . .
on land soon to be part of the Mississippi Territory.
Another home for Glasgow.
Once again,
he packed his belongings.

His father had a new job: helping to settle Pascagoula.
A courier,
he carried letters to officials in West Florida,
owned by Spain . . .
or sailed to New Orleans,
taking Glasgow on his trips across the Mississippi Sound
where the boy spotted the landmark
all good sailors looked for on the horizon . . .

Ship Island!

The seven-mile sandspit, in the shape of a ship,
had a bay with deep water,
safe for anchoring,
the only one in the shallow sound.

Then, at the farm in Pascagoula . . .

like a bend in the Mississippi River,
Glasgow Farragut's life turned.

One day,
Commander David Porter left the naval station
and sailed across the sound to visit George Farragut.
He knew it was hard for his father's friend
to care for three children and a baby,
and Porter had an offer . . .
if George's second son, Glasgow, was willing.

The officer told the boy
he and his wife Evelina wanted to be his guardians.
They wouldn't *adopt* him,
but Glasgow could live with them in New Orleans.
The Porters also wanted to take Nancy into their home.
For Glasgow,
his family was the center of his world.

But David Porter promised he could visit Pascagoula . . .
and Nancy would be with him in New Orleans.
When Glasgow was old enough,
Commander Porter would help him join the navy
and go to sea.

The navy! To sea!

WINTER 1809

Glasgow Farragut later wrote:
"I, being inspired by his uniform
and that of my brother William . . .
said promptly that I would go."

And so Glasgow and Nancy began a new life . . .
with David and Evelina Porter in New Orleans . . .
who cared for both as their own,
even after a son, named William Porter,
was born in March.

There were visits to Pascagoula,
and Glasgow still sailed with his father George
on Lake Pontchartrain . . .
where on the deck of a boat,
he always found adventure.

Sailing!

Over the next months,
his guardian became Glasgow's friend,
mentor,
and teacher.

David Porter was a confident commander,
and at the naval station,
sailors were well trained,
and ships were ready to sail.
Glasgow was intrigued by Porter's code book,
with lists of signal flags to use,

so the gunboats in New Orleans
could exchange messages when on patrol.

The boy tagged behind his guardian
and watched as the flags
were raised and lowered.
For the rest of his life,
these would fascinate him.

Pages from David Porter's 1809 signal book, written while Porter commanded the New Orleans naval station

SPRING 1810

David Porter kept his promise.

In 1810,
a year after James Madison was sworn in
as America's president,
Glasgow's name was added to the muster roll
at the New Orleans naval station:

J. G. Farragut, Boy,
12 April, 1810, to 15 June, 1810.

Earning wages for his work, a total of thirteen dollars,
by helping where a small boy could help . . .
James Glasgow Farragut,
at age eight,
was the youngest ever to be paid by the US Navy.

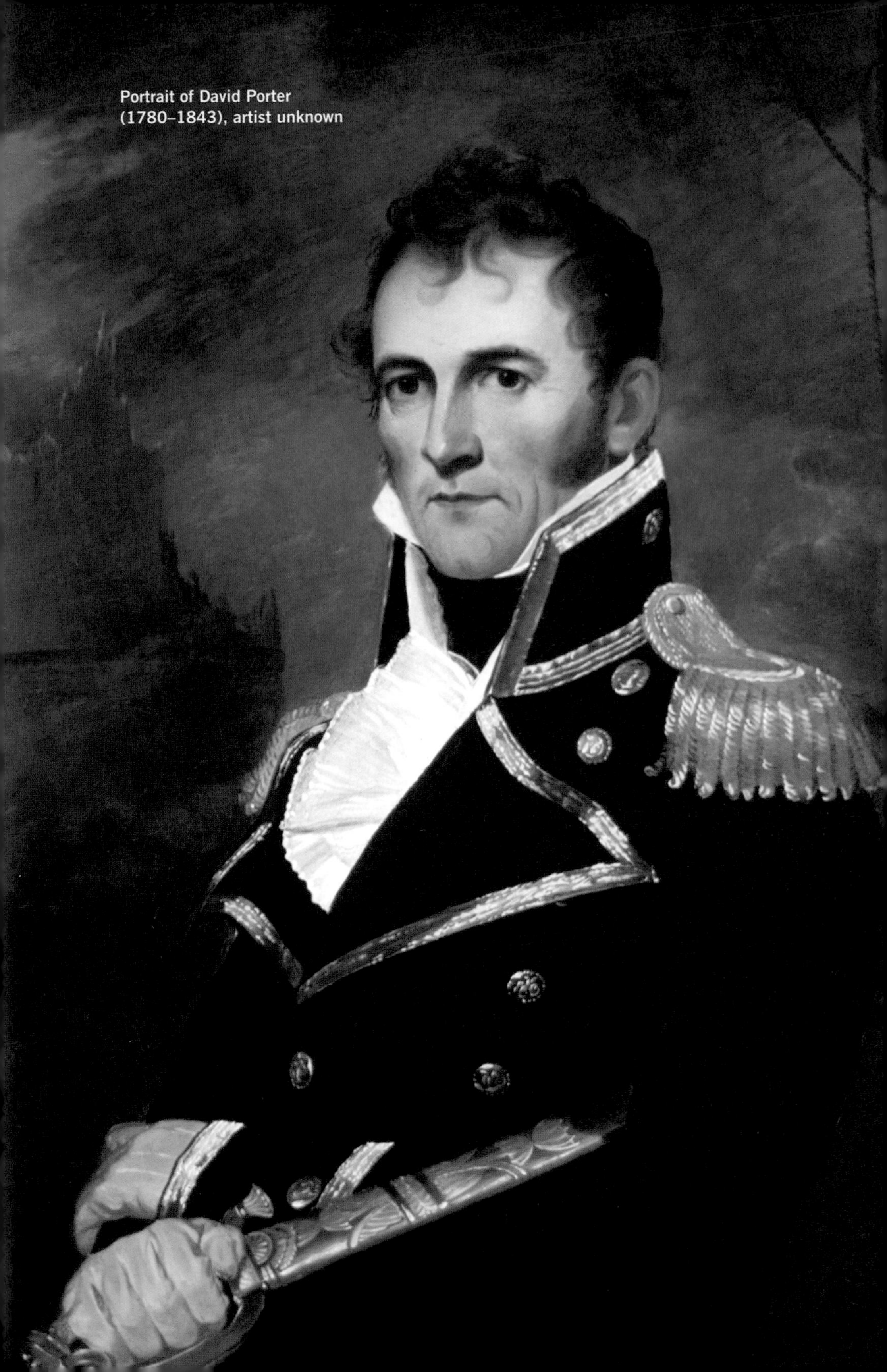

Portrait of David Porter
(1780–1843), artist unknown

SUMMER 1810

That June,
the Department of the Navy ordered David Porter
to leave the naval station
and report to Washington.
He and Evelina decided Nancy Farragut, now six,
should stay in New Orleans,
near Pascagoula,
so she could visit her real papa, George.
David Porter's sister,
who lived in New Orleans,
took over as Nancy's guardian.

Glasgow said goodbye to his family at the farm . . .
and with the Porters and little William,
boarded the *Vesuvius*,
a navy ketch with a main mast and a mizzen mast,
armed with mortars in the bow.

Ketch.

K-e-t-c-h.

What a ship!

The United States Navy!

James Madison was often called the "Father of the
Constitution" and served as president from 1809–1817.
This portrait was painted by Thomas Sully in 1809.

Glasgow listened to the whistle of the bosun's silver pipe,
and when the anchor was raised,
heard the call *Anchors aweigh!*
which meant the ship was moving through the water.
As sailors stood in the rigging
and the wind puffed out the slack sails,
he counted a crew of thirty men.
After a stop in Havana, Cuba,
the *Vesuvius* headed north . . .
into the windy Atlantic.
The sun shone on a horizon of blue,
and Glasgow couldn't stop looking up, up
at the ship's white canvas wings.

The Atlantic Ocean!

On July 5,
the boy, short in stature but agile and quick,
saluted his birthday by doing a handspring on deck.

Nine! On a bomb ketch!

Days later,
the *Vesuvius* tacked into the Chesapeake Bay
and sailed up the Potomac and Anacostia Rivers,
to Washington with its mud avenues
and President's House where James Madison lived.
Always curious,
Glasgow studied the shore
as the ketch dropped anchor on July 23
in the Anacostia
at the Washington Navy Yard . . .
much bigger than the station in New Orleans.

City of Washington from Beyond the Navy Yard, painted in 1833 by George Cooke, shows the Anacostia River. This painting has hung in the Oval Office of the White House under Presidents Ford, Carter, Reagan, Clinton, Obama, and Biden.

Built in 1799,
on land chosen by President Washington,
the Navy Yard was the first and oldest
naval station in the country.
And David Porter, who knew it well,
showed Glasgow around the docks and sheds
that thrummed with the work
of America's sailors.

During the next months,
while Porter attended naval meetings,
Glasgow went to school each morning.
Reading. Writing. Spelling.
His head spun with words and numbers . . .
but he knew not every boy or girl had such a chance.

One day,
Commander Porter took Glasgow to see
Paul Hamilton,
the secretary of the navy.

The head of the navy!

Glasgow stood as tall as he could next to his guardian.
He wanted to *be* David Porter ...
worldly and kind ...
a reader,
a writer,
an artist,
and a commander of a ship.
When the secretary shook the boy's hand
and promised to send him a warrant
after he turned ten,
Glasgow knew a life in the navy
was all he wanted.

Midshipman!

Someday ...

In late autumn, the Porter family
boarded the *Vesuvius*
and sailed down the Potomac
to the Chesapeake Bay
into the Atlantic and north
to the Delaware River ...
and up to Green Bank,
one of the finest houses
in Chester, Pennsylvania.

This portrait of Paul Hamilton
(1762–1816) is by G. B. Matthews.
In 1809 Hamilton was appointed
by President Madison to serve as
the third secretary of the navy. From
South Carolina, he fought in the
War for Independence under
General Francis Marion.

Green Bank was drawn in 1882 by David Stauffer based on a sketch done in 1827 by J. F. Watson. Located at Second and Welsh Streets in Chester, the mansion was destroyed in an explosion in 1882.

After the *Vesuvius* anchored,
Glasgow went ashore with the Porters
in the ship's wherry, a small rowboat.
Green Bank had a view of the river
and Glasgow watched ships passing by,
sailing north to Philadelphia,
twenty miles away.
Candlesticks,
books,
a desk for the commander . . .
a table for Glasgow's schoolwork . . .
it was all astonishing to a boy
who'd grown up in the Tennessee woods.

Glasgow saw the world opening to him.
The Porters were his family
And Green Bank was his home.
This was his life.

FALL 1810

In Chester,
Glasgow was again a student.

A slate and a piece of chalk.
Geography.
Numbers . . . not always easy.
After his studies,
Glasgow played outdoors with his classmates . . .
or with William Porter, still a toddler,
who now had a baby sister, Elizabeth.

And always,
he dreamed of his future.

That December,
news came from Washington.
Secretary Hamilton hadn't waited
for Glasgow Farragut to turn ten.
On the seventeenth,
his commission as a midshipman had been signed . . .

by President Madison.

JAMES MADISON, PRESIDENT OF THE UNITED STATES OF AMERICA. To all who shall see these presents, GREETINGS: KNOW YE, That reposing special Trust and Confidence in the Patriotism, Valour, Fidelity and Abilities of GLASGOW FARRAGUT I do appoint him a Midshipman in the NAVY OF THE UNITED STATES:

He is therefore carefully and diligently to discharge the duties of a Midshipman by doing and performing all manner of things thereunto belonging. And I do strictly charge and require all Officers, Seamen and others, under his command, to be obedient to his orders as a Midshipman. And he is to observe and follow such orders and directions, from time to time, as he shall receive from me, or the future President of the United States of America, or his superior officer set over him, according to the Rules and Discipline of the Navy. This Warrant to continue in force during the pleasure of the President of the United States for the time being. GIVEN under my Hand, at the City of Washington, this seventeenth day of December in the year of our Lord one Thousand eight hundred and ten and in the thirty-fourth year of the Independence of the United States.

JAMES MADISON

By the President.
Paul Hamilton

Midshipman!

> I, Glasgow Farragut appointed Midshipman in the Navy of the United States do solemnly swear to bear true allegiance to the United States of America, and to serve them honestly and faithfully against all their enemies or opposers whomsoever; and to observe and obey the orders of the President of the United States of America, and the orders of the officers appointed over me, and in all things to conform myself to the rules and regulations which now are or hereafter may be directed, and to the articles of war which may be enacted by Congress, for the better government of the navy of the United States, and that I will support the constitution of the United States.
>
> SWORN BEFORE ME,
>
> Chester Dec 19th 1810   G. Farragut
>
> Isaac Eyre justice of the Peace in the County of Delaware State of Pennsylvania

At age nine,
Glasgow had a path to follow in the US Navy.
With his *patriotism* . . . love of country,
with his *valor* . . . courage in danger,
with his *fidelity* . . . faithfulness,
and with his *abilities* . . . talents and skills.

Two days later, Glasgow wrote G. Farragut
on his own warrant,
with a promise he hoped to keep all his life . . .

to bear true allegiance
to the United States of America,
and to serve them . . .
against all their enemies.

Glasgow *knew* he was the luckiest boy
to have David Porter as his champion
and thought about the name he'd had since birth:
James Glasgow Farragut.

David Glasgow Farragut was the name he now wanted
even though his guardian, to the end of his life,
would call him Glasgow.

To celebrate the warrant and honor their friendship,
David Porter,
who loved Glasgow like a younger brother,
gave him a gold watch
engraved with his new initials:
   DP to DGF
     U.S.N.
     1810
On its ribbon was the commander's portrait
to use as a seal.
Glasgow held the watch with care
and tried to find words to thank his guardian.

U.S.N.
United States Navy.

He knew each time he used the watch,
it would remind him of David Porter,
his friend and protector.

Glasgow's watch, with the red seal containing David Porter's portrait, is on display at the United States Naval Academy Museum in Annapolis, Maryland.

Note the initials for Farragut's new name.

That winter,
in his room at Green Bank,
Glasgow tried on his dress uniform
with its blue jacket and white vest and breeches.
His uniform.
He touched the dagger . . . known as a dirk,
that he'd wear on his belt aboard ship
and the button and lace on his collar.

Midshipman!

Glasgow couldn't wait to sleep in a ship's hammock.
And see a foreign port.
And salute his captain.
And serve the United States of America.

Midshipman . . .
then lieutenant . . .
then commander . . .
then captain.

David G. Farragut.
This was the name he'd take from Green Bank
into his future.

THE MIDSHIPMAN

2

APPOINTED
DECEMBER 17, 1810
BY PRESIDENT JAMES MADISON

SUMMER 1811

Months later . . . in early August,
at the naval station in Norfolk, Virginia,
Mr. Farragut,
as he was to be called as a midshipman,
boarded the frigate *Essex*
with a note to Lieutenant John Downes, the officer in charge,
from Commander Porter.
Mr. Farragut was to direct the wherry
that would row Porter to the *Essex*, his new command.
Already, his guardian trusted Glasgow as a leader.

The *Essex*, like other frigates,
had been built to make the US Navy stronger.
Because in 1811,
it was dangerous for any American ship
to sail in the Atlantic.
The British were in a war . . . with France.
The United States hadn't taken sides,
but since the British needed men in their navy,
they stopped vessels on the seas
and dragged sailors off their ships.
Americans had been *impressed*, forced to join British crews.

Having just turned ten, with his birthday handspring,
Mr. Farragut pondered the injustice of this . . .
and was indignant.

He'd heard his guardian talk about the British actions . . .
and he knew President Madison had sent letters,
asking for respect on the sea.
But America's sailors were *still* being impressed.
And Great Britain's King George III claimed lands near Canada
that belonged to the US were *his*.

Under clouds of a future war . . .
that August day Mr. Farragut stared in awe at the *Essex*
for the first time.
Designed to carry thirty-six guns,
she was armed with ten more;
forty were *carronades*,
short-range cannon for close combat.
Above the waterline,
a pale stripe ran along her black hull
and framed the port and starboard gun ports.
Each could be opened to fire on an enemy
or closed to hide the muzzle of its gun.

As he walked along the gun deck
to count and touch the carronades,
Mr. Farragut felt the *power* of his ship.

The frigate *Essex* with cannon ports visible was painted by artist Joseph Howard (1789–1857). The ship was built in 1799 in Salem, Massachusetts, where farmers carried timbers across the snow on sleds to the harbor. Copper fittings were supplied by Paul Revere.

The *Essex* was already famous . . .
a few years before,
she'd sailed around the Cape of Good Hope
into the Indian Ocean,
the *first* American warship to do so.

The *Vesuvius* had been manned by a crew of thirty.
But on the *Essex*,
David Porter commanded *three hundred and twenty-five men* . . .
gunners, cooks, seamen, carpenters,
sailmakers, surgeons, officers,
marines who could fight on land and sea,
bosuns, and more.
Of the ship's twelve midshipmen,
Mr. Farragut was the youngest and the smallest.

Mr. Farragut began his duties
and soon carried messages to and from
the decks of the frigate . . .
the open top deck or *spar deck,*
the gun deck,
and others.

Each midshipman was assigned to a group of gunners,
a division,
to make sure all were present . . .
and carried powder to them in drills.
Farragut "took the sun" to measure the ship's latitude,
saluted officers,
climbed into the rigging like a cat
to help seamen adjust the sails . . .
went to classes on navigation taught by the chaplain . . .
and tagged behind his favorite lieutenants,
Downes, William Finch, and now a good friend, John Cowell,
who, like wise older brothers,
looked after the midshipmen.

Day or night,
Mr. Farragut and his comrades had orders
to stand watch . . .
which meant keeping the ship safe
by patrolling one of the decks
like a sentry on guard.

On the *Essex*,
there were three watches . . .
each was eight hours long.

There were few lanterns to light the darkness
and on one cold watch
Mr. Farragut blinked and blinked
as he leaned against a gun-carriage . . .
must stay awake . . . must stay awake
but his eyelids kept closing.
And closing.

When Lieutenant Finch, on the same watch,
passed by the sleeping boy,
he remembered Farragut's age
and took off his own jacket
and carried the midshipman to his hammock.

Some seamen joked about his height . . .
but when Mr. Farragut climbed into the rigging
without a trace of fear to scan the horizon,
he earned their respect.
From the masts or the rope shrouds,
he could see sunshine on the waves . . .
shimmering in dots of light.
Or see changes in the depth of the water.

Dawns and sunsets painted the shallows
orange or pink or blue.
High in the rigging was where he wanted to be.

If David Porter couldn't find the boy he still called Glasgow,
he knew to look up.

SPRING 1812

By the late spring of 1812,
the United States was on the brink of war with Great Britain.

In the past five years,
more than six thousand American sailors
had been impressed,
so after anger and talk, Congress took a vote . . .
seventy-nine *for war* and forty-nine *against war*
in the House
and nineteen *for* war and thirteen *against* war
in the Senate.

On June 18, 1812,
President Madison made an official declaration.

War!

Mr. Farragut's eleventh birthday was just weeks away.

War!

On the *Essex,*
David Porter gave a patriotic speech,
and for three days in a row,
the crew lined up to repeat an oath of allegiance
to the country.

SUMMER 1812

On July 2,
just before taking the *Essex* back to sea with new orders,
Porter was promoted to *captain*.
Mr. Farragut's eyes shone with pride for his guardian.
Captain Porter.
The highest rank!

A day later,
David Porter ordered the capstan near the stern
turned to raise the anchor.
The sails of the *Essex* billowed with wind,
and the ship put to sea.
Another day later,
young Farragut felt a happy shiver
when he heard his ship salute the United States
by firing guns at sunrise, noon, and sunset.

The United States. His country.

And on July 5, his birthday,
Mr. Farragut, circled by his midshipmen friends,
did a handspring on the spar deck
to celebrate.

He might be small but always, he was quick and fit.

War!

Each day,
the midshipmen saw Captain Porter command his ship
and train his crew to be in *fighting trim,*
ready for *any* battle ahead.
Sailors sharpened their cutlasses
and were drilled on boarding an enemy ship.
Gunners cleaned and checked the carronades.
Decks were scrubbed and charts were checked.

Sea battles lay ahead with a powerful enemy.
The US Navy had *less than twenty* actual warships . . .
the British navy had more than *five hundred.*
America had *five thousand* sailors and officers . . .
Great Britain had more than *one hundred and fifty thousand.*

As Mr. Farragut watched David Porter
take his ship from a time of peace
to a time of war,
he knew *this* was the kind of captain
he wanted to become.

In August,
the *Essex* sailed north
to waters near Newfoundland to hunt British ships . . .
often taking down her top sails
to disguise herself as an unarmed merchant vessel.

On the thirteenth,
while Mr. Farragut was at his post on deck . . .

Sail ho!

A British sail!

The call stirred the Americans on the *Essex*.
To trick the enemy and with speed,
Porter's crew closed the gunports,
lowered the Stars and Stripes,
and raised the British flag.
Posing as a trader,
the *Essex* lured the ship on the horizon,
the *Alert,*
to come closer.
And closer.

Calling off their names
Mr. Farragut stood with his gun division
as men slid open the ports . . .
click by click.

Farragut saw a mate hoist the American flag,
and the *Essex* gunners took aim
at the enemy ship.
When the British sloop fired at the *Essex* with scattered shots,
Captain Porter gave the order to fire the carronades
in a broadside.
Boom! BOOM!
Amid the smoke and flames,
the *Alert* surrendered after only an eight-minute battle.

Porter sent his carpenters to board his prize
and plug her holes,
and the *Alert* was taken in tow . . .
the first ship to be captured by the US Navy in this war,
along with eighty-six British sailors.
Mr. Farragut stood near David Porter
and watched lines of prisoners
file aboard the *Essex*
as his crewmates swaggered with the victory.

The capture of the HMS *Alert* by the USS *Essex* in 1812 from the book *Our Country in War*, written and illustrated by Murat Halstead in 1898. HMS stands for His (or Her) Majesty's Ship.

But the *Alert*'s men plotted trouble
aboard the *Essex*.

In his hammock on the night of August 18,
Farragut was awakened by the soft sound of footsteps.
Pretending to be asleep,
the boy saw through half-closed eyes
a British sailor, gun in hand, watching him.
Then the man moved on past.

The prisoners meant to take over the Essex!

Mr. Farragut rolled from his hammock
and crept through the dark ship
to David Porter's quarters to wake and warn his captain . . .
who loudly called *Fire! Fire!* . . .
so his crew,
who had practiced night drills,
would rush to their posts.
Which they did . . . in minutes.
Farragut's action and courage
had saved his ship from the British plotters
and Porter's crew quelled the trouble.

From then on,
the midshipman trusted himself to take bold action
in spite of danger.

FALL 1812

The *Essex* returned to the Delaware River
for a short stay,
as Captain Porter awaited secret wartime orders
from the Department of the Navy.
The ships in America's fleet
were to be divided into squadrons,
or groups,
to hunt the British on the seas.

David Porter knew that, soon,
he'd be away from his family for months.
On October 28 at Green Bank,
after hugging Evelina and the two Porter children,
Glasgow and his guardian boarded the wherry.

Evelina Anderson Porter (1790–1871) and a daughter. The Porter family would grow to ten children, not including David Glasgow Farragut. Four (William, David Dixon, Thomas, and Hambleton) of six Porter sons served in the US Navy.

The capstan on the *Essex* was turned,
Anchors aweigh!
and the frigate sailed south to the Atlantic
with orders to meet two other ships,
the *Constitution* and the *Hornet.*
The squadron would sail to the Cape Verde Islands
near Africa,
then tack back to the coast of Brazil
to look for British vessels . . .
or sail on to the Pacific
and knock out the British whaling fleet there.

Due to bad weather,
the *Essex* was a few days late
and sailed alone to the meeting place
in Cape Verde.
Once there,
Porter found the other two ships had left for Brazil.
On December 2,
to keep his warship's next destination a secret,
he ordered the *Essex* to sail *south* toward Africa
and then, when she was out of sight of land,
to turn *west* toward Brazil.
Again, once there,
lookouts on the *Essex* never spotted
the *Constitution* or the *Hornet.*
So Captain Porter chose to sail on alone . . .
to the Pacific.

His dream was to explore the South American coast
and islands to the west.
He'd even written a letter to President Jefferson
about his hopes.
Now, years later, he would have his chance.
The *Essex* could raid the British whalers
that fished off the coast of Chile . . .
and *destroy* their rich trade
that sent money back to England to fund the war.
Porter's plan was to *capture* these whaling ships,
live off their supplies,
and sell the cargoes of blubber and oil
in South America's ports.

Before sailing anywhere,
the *Essex* needed to restock with food,
thousands of gallons of water,
and what every ship carried:
lemons and limes to prevent scurvy.
All midshipmen knew the health of a crew
was as important as training.
Scurvy can kill a sailor . . . best eat those bitter limes.

In a Brazilian port,
Mr. Farragut called out orders,
checked lists,
and took charge as barrels were loaded onto his ship.
Along the coast,
some of the crew bought monkeys and parrots
and brought them aboard as pets.

After the *Essex* weighed anchor and sailed south
to the tip of South America,
Farragut saw the habits of a true leader
each time he visited his guardian's cabin
where Porter wrote in his journal,
sketched,
studied maps,
and drew up plans with his lieutenants.
And the boy knew that on Porter's desk,
near the code book of signal flags
he'd been allowed to page through,
were charts ... drawn by seamen
who had visited the Galápagos Islands.

WINTER 1813

In early February,
David Porter told his crew
they were headed where some had guessed . . .
to the Pacific.

The Pacific!

Young Farragut tried to imagine
this vast ocean where *no* American warship
had ever sailed before.
The crew knew their ship would be alone,
in wartime . . .
as she cruised into unknown waters.
All the men aboard trusted their captain.
Mr. Farragut knew his guardian
favored longer-range guns
more than the *Essex*'s carronades.
Yet, the *Essex* was ready . . . for *any* trouble.
No one knew if American soldiers were in battle
on land back home.
Ahead of the frigate was water . . . and sky.

And so, the course was set.

Cape Horn . . .
at the tip of South America,
where the Atlantic Ocean met the Pacific.
Mr. Farragut listened with a chill
as older sailors spun stories of terrible winds
and churning seas.

Captain David Porter had never sailed there
but he was a man of preparation.
Guns were stored below
and topmasts and sails taken down.
Then after gusts and high waves,
a few weeks later,
lookouts sighted the Horn with its rocky cliffs.
Mr. Farragut and those on the *Essex* wore woolen clothes
that were never dry . . .
and only officers wore shoes.
Soon black clouds pounced on the *Essex*
and winds swept freezing rain across the days.

The sea broke through the gunports,
and washed sailors from their hammocks.
Now shivering men suffered from frostbite.
Towering waves battered the *Essex*.
Storms tore at the sails and clawed at the masts
and terror began to spread from sailor to sailor
as the ship ran low on food and water.

Porter cut each man's rations in half
and prayed the storms would blow past.
Bruised from falls,
he moved from deck to deck,
calling orders to his crew.

"The sea [increased] to such a height
as to threaten to swallow us each instance;
the whole ocean was a continuous foam of breakers.
The heaviest squall I have ever before experienced,
has not equaled in violence
the most moderate intervals of this hurricane,"
the captain recorded in his journal.

On each dark day,
Farragut and the other eleven midshipmen,
their faces frozen with fear,
clung to the lines on the frigate's decks
as walls of saltwater smacked against them.
When the storms tore into the sails,
Porter's navigator and officers at the helm
tried to keep the ship from being swamped
but with the sun and the moon
always hidden,
they had no idea of the ship's location
or direction.

Farragut heard the wails and prayers of his crewmates
as men sobbed on deck
and begged God for mercy.
Dizzy from hunger,
Mr. Farragut tried to calm his own panic
when he heard wood splinter
and guns slam below the deck.

Will I perish, God?

Sailors ate their parrots and monkeys
rather than starve.

The boy was inspired by his lieutenant heroes,
Downes, Finch, and Cowell,
and always Captain Porter
whose steady voice helped men overcome their fear
and return to their posts.

Finally,
the weeks of gales ebbed like a tide.
The *Essex* limped into the Pacific,
miraculously having lost only a few sails
and timbers.
David Porter inspected his ship
and cheered on each sailor.

On March 5,
albatrosses . . . large seabirds . . .
soared above the ship, a sign of land nearby,
and at the meridian,
the crew saw snow-topped mountains, the Andes,
in the distance.

One of the largest flying birds in the world, the albatross can have a wingspan of almost
twelve feet, live up to fifty years, and travel thousands of miles in a single journey.
This black-browed albatross flies near the coast of Chile. Some sailors saw albatrosses
as signs of good luck. Others thought they were the souls of sailors lost at sea.

Mr. Farragut put the awful days behind him
like a bad dream
and felt the sun on his face as he went about his duties
and with his friends,
returned to the classes on navigation.
Carpenters set to their repairs . . .
while the sailmakers patched the canvas
and David Porter and the chaplain
gathered the crew on deck to give thanks to God.

The captain and his sailors were proud of their sturdy ship . . .
the *Essex* was the *first warship*
flying an American flag to ever round Cape Horn.
Rich British prizes were out there . . .
and Porter promised his crew they would find them.

USS *Essex* rounding Cape Horn, artist unknown

SPRING AND SUMMER 1813

To encourage his men,
David Porter had a reminder of *why* the United States was at war.
As the *Essex* prowled the Pacific coast
of South America,
on the hunt for British whaling ships,
the words *Free Trade and Sailors Rights*
rippled on a banner
next to the American flag that flew from the mast.

Without news,
Porter could only hope soldiers and sailors at home
were taking the fight to the British.
If peace came,
the ships of the United States
could trade on safe seas
and her sailors would no longer be impressed.

Quickly,
the *Essex* found the British whaling fleet,
schooners with small crews and few guns.
Porter's sailors took down her white banner
and US flag,
and raised a British or Spanish flag
to trick the enemy and sail close to them.
The black American warship
could outgun whalers in any fight.

Each time,
Mr. Farragut carried messages . . .
or hurried with powder to his gun group,
skittering across the *Essex* gun deck
to supply the men at their carronades.
And watched when the British surrendered.

Porter took their vessels, which he called *prize ships*, in tow
or had his own men sail them.
Soon he had a fleet,
along with a captured whaler, the *Barclay*.
It was time to rest and smoke out rats from the ships.
The *Essex* and her prizes headed to the Galápagos Islands
where Mr. Farragut saw an amazing sight . . .

The Galápagos giant tortoise can live for a hundred years or more. The old Spanish word *galápago* means "tortoise." During their stay in the Galápagos Islands, the crew of the USS *Essex* ate the meat from these tortoises.

Giant tortoises!

That June,
as they explored the islands,
Captain Porter assigned some prize ships
to his officers,
led by Lieutenant Downes.
They would sail them two thousand miles
down the coast to Valparaiso in Chile . . .
where it was safe for American ships to anchor
since Chile took no side in this war.
Porter had written letters home to Evelina
and reports to the secretary of the navy . . .
Downes would take these with him
and send them on through officials
to Washington.

Mr. Farragut was almost twelve,
and David Porter trusted him to lead men,
so he assigned the boy to Downes's group
and gave him command of the *Barclay*.

"I was sent as prize-master to the Barclay.
This was an important event in my life . . .
I was to take the ship to Valparaiso,
I felt . . . pride at finding myself in command
at twelve years of age. . . . I was to control the men
sent from our frigate,
while the Captain was to navigate the vessel,"
the midshipman recorded in a later journal.

On July 8,
Porter and the *Essex* returned north to the Galápagos Islands,
while Downes's squadron of prize ships tacked south.
The *Barclay*'s whaling captain balked and mocked Mr. Farragut
in front of the crew . . .
refusing to let his ship be commanded by a *boy*.
Fearless, Farragut stood on the deck
and ordered the captain to his cabin.
Then he called to sailors in the rigging
to fill the topsail.

Aye, aye, sir! came the reply.

With the midshipman in command,
the *Barclay* sailed on for two thousand miles,
and safely reached Valparaiso.

FALL 1813

After taking Captain Porter's letters to Valparaiso,
Downes left the *Barclay* in the harbor,
sold the other prize ships,
and with Farragut aboard,
sailed back to the Galápagos
on a vessel they had renamed the *Essex Junior*.

They arrived on September 30,
at the meridian,
and Captain Porter was pleased to see them.
Soon both ships, with a few captured whalers,
charted a course west, three thousand miles,
to the Marquesas Islands.

"These were among the happiest days
of my life,"
Midshipman Farragut later wrote.

The archipelago was exotic
and when they reached Nuku Hiva,
the largest of the twelve islands,
where the *Essex*, the *Essex Junior*, and their prize ships
anchored in its bay,
Farragut made friends with Marquesan boys and girls
who taught him to throw a spear . . .
walk on stilts . . .
and become a strong swimmer.

WINTER 1814

But when news came to Captain Porter
in the Marquesas
that a British squadron had come to the Pacific
and was hunting the *Essex*,
he sailed his ship back to Valparaiso,
and Lieutenant Downes followed in the *Essex Junior*.

Two of the enemy's warships were there . . .
the frigate *Phoebe*, with more guns than the *Essex*,
and a smaller ship, the *Cherub* . . .
waiting to pounce on the American ship
as soon as she left the neutral harbor
to sail on the open sea.
A game of waiting began
and on the harbor docks,
British sailors taunted the officers of the *Essex*
who called back *Free Trade and Sailors Rights*.
After six weeks of being trapped in the safe harbor,
David Porter decided to try to slip out to sea
and head home.

SPRING AND SUMMER 1814

On March 28,
the *Essex* quietly left the harbor and put to sea
when a sudden squall hit her, with high winds,
and tore off her topmast.

Captain Porter sailed her into the shelter of a bay
but the *Essex* drifted near the shore,
like a wounded bird without wings.
Mr. Farragut and others watched
as the British ships, alerted to her peril,
sailed toward her,
cutting off any escape.
The *Essex* was soon attacked . . .
with withering fire from broadsides by the *Phoebe*
whose guns had a longer range
than the carronades on Porter's ship.
The American crew was aghast.
All knew the *Essex* guns couldn't reach her foes.

That afternoon,
the *Phoebe*'s deadly salvos hammered the *Essex*.
Mr. Farragut rushed across the bloody decks,
helping his mates or taking orders from David Porter.
"I shall never forget the horrid impression
made upon me at the sight of the first man
I had ever seen killed. . . .
But they soon began to fall around me so fast
that it all appeared like a dream,"
the midshipman later recorded.

Painting of the capture of the USS *Essex* by the HMS *Phoebe* and HMS *Cherub*, attributed to George Ropes, Jr. (1788–1819) from Salem, Massachusetts, who, at age nineteen, used his artistic talent to support his eight siblings after his father died at sea.

Screams of anguish filled the air
as the battle raged,
and Farragut's good friend, Lieutenant Cowell,
was badly wounded.
Writhing in pain, he cheered on his shipmates.
The noise of the British guns and the carronades
that answered back filled the burning deck.

Knocked down a ladder by a blast,
and badly bruised,
Farragut hurried to the upper deck
to assist his captain.
Half of his *Essex* crewmates were killed—*killed!*—
or wounded.
Some jumped off the ship and drowned.

The proud David Porter knew his ship's guns
were outmatched.
The *Essex* was in flames . . .
and his only choice was surrender.
Quickly he ordered Mr. Farragut to find the signal book
and throw it into the sea
to keep its secrets from the enemy.
Amid the smoke and noise,
the twelve-year-old ran to the captain's cabin . . .
and then searched one of the decks
until he finally found the code book
on a ledge near one of the gunports.

Seizing it,
he threw the book into the sea
that was filled with the debris of battle:
coats, barrels, torn sails,
and the floating bodies of his crewmates.
As Porter surrendered the ship,
the small midshipman and a crewmate
zigzagged across the burning decks,
gathering pistols lost in the carnage,
and lobbed them into the water
to keep them from the enemy.

After the surrender,
Porter, his crew, and his officers became prisoners
of the British.
Captain James Hillyar, who commanded the *Phoebe*,
held the Americans in Valparaiso.
The next morning,
meeting the British captain,
Farragut wept at the capture of his ship.

During the next days,
the heartbroken boy worked from morning to night
helping the surgeon of the *Essex*.
"I rose at daylight
and arranged the bandages
and plasters until 8 a.m.;
then, after breakfast,
I went to work at my patients,"
Farragut wrote later.

War was *real*...
and the *Essex* and many of his friends,
among them Lieutenant Cowell,
who died in Valparaiso after surgery,
had been torn from his life.
In late April,
Captain Porter and those of his crew who were alive
left on their long trip home aboard the *Essex Junior*,
now a British ship.

They arrived in New York City on July 5, 1814.

It was David Glasgow Farragut's thirteenth birthday,
and he was a prisoner of the British,
soon to be exchanged for an enemy prisoner
and set free.

As a midshipman
on his first official US Navy cruise,
he'd sailed
almost twenty-seven thousand miles...
and seen death choose others.
With his captain, David Porter,
he headed *home*... to Chester.

A year earlier,
Evelina had given birth to another son,
David Dixon Porter,
when her husband was away on the *Essex*.

John Evans,	17 December,	1810.
Alexander Eskridge,	1 January,	1812.
Frank Ellery,	do.	do.
Samuel A. Eakin,	18 June,	do.
Charles Ellery,	8 March,	1814.
Christopher T. Emmet,	1 October,	do.
Frederick Engle,	6 December,	do.
Ambrose Field,	1 December,	1809.
David G. Farragut,	17 do.	1810.
French Forrest,	9 June,	1811.
Andrew Fitzhugh,	do.	do.
Edgar Freeman,	do.	do.
Robert Field,	1 September,	do.
John D. Fischer,	18 June,	1812.
T. W. Freelon,	do.	do.
Thomas E. Finnemore,	20 February,	1813.
James M. Freeman,	24 May,	1814.

Page from the register of the US Navy, 1814, that lists David Farragut as a midshipman with the date of his commission

The bold captain,
hailed as a hero even with the loss of his ship,
didn't stay at Green Bank for long.
Leaving his midshipman and his family,
Porter headed south in a ship with orders
from the secretary of the navy
to help defend Washington.

But he was too late to be of aid.
The British had won a battle on August 24
in Bladensburg, Maryland,
scattering American soldiers
who didn't regroup to defend the capital.
President Madison, his wife, and Congress
had fled Washington for safety.

That evening,
the enemy made a quick attack
and set fires in the city . . .
revenge for the burning by American soldiers
of York, a town in Canada, a year before.

The US Capitol Building and the President's House
were in flames.
And the Navy Yard was burning also . . .
on orders of the secretary of the navy
to keep it from the British.

BRITISH BURN THE CAPITOL · 1814

Allyn Cox painted this mural in the House wing of the Capitol in 1974. It shows
the burning of the Capitol by the British in 1814.

FALL 1814 TO 1820

In September . . . while David Glasgow Farragut
was safe at Green Bank in Chester . . .
the British sailed north to Baltimore,
an important port and a bigger prize than Washington.
This time the Americans were ready
and the sturdy star-shaped walls of Fort McHenry
in the inner harbor
held against the fierce fire by British ships
of a thousand rockets, mortars, and bombs.
The defeated enemy sailed away . . .
south to attack another big port, New Orleans.

Before *that* battle, in Louisiana,
which the United States won . . .
a peace treaty between the two nations
was signed on December 24, 1814, in Ghent, Belgium.
The fight with the British ended in early 1815.
After the US Senate voted in February to ratify the treaty
and President Madison signed it,
peace came to the high seas.

And young Farragut,
carrying his gold watch in his pocket,
stepped into his future with the United States Navy,
serving the country he loved.

British ships attacked Fort McHenry in Baltimore's harbor on September 13 and 14, 1814. Our national anthem, "The Star-Spangled Banner," based on this battle won by Americans, was written as a poem on September 14 by Francis Scott Key, who witnessed the bombardment.

On his tours of duty,
he sailed to the Mediterranean.
To the Caribbean.
To the Chesapeake.
To the Mediterranean again.
To the Atlantic.
To the Gulf of Mexico.
To bays and ports and islands.

No officer his age had sailed as many miles.
As a midshipman,
David Farragut often served as an aide
to the captain of his ship,
always observing the skills of a leader.

In a journal as a teenager,
he recorded his travels . . .
writing details in his slanted script
with a quill pen and ink.

About the harbors he visited.
About the pirate ships he hunted.
About the fevers that made him ill.
About the people he met.
About the forts of other countries.
About the coasts he patrolled.
About the storms he sailed through.

And when aboard the *Washington*, in 1817,
during months in the Mediterranean,
he wrote about his friendship with Charles Folsom,
who became his mentor
when the chaplain became an American consul
in North Africa.
"I resided in Tunis for nine months,
pursuing my studies under Mr. Folsom. . . .
I studied French, Italian, English literature,
and mathematics,"
Farragut penned in his notebook.

At age sixteen during a desert outing,
the midshipman was stricken by sunstroke
and almost blinded.
For the rest of his life,
Farragut's eyes were so weak
he often asked others to pen his letters
or read to him
since he could only study or write one page at a time.

USS *Independence*, painted in 1981 by Rear Admiral J. W. Schmidt, was the first American "ship of the line," ready for battle with seventy-four guns. As a midshipman, David Farragut sailed to the Mediterranean for the first time, aboard the *Independence*, in April of 1815. A year later, he returned to duty in the Mediterranean aboard the USS *Washington*.

In 1816, Midshipman Farragut returned to duty in the Mediterranean on the USS *Washington*, launched in Portsmouth, New Hampshire, in 1814. The ship was later painted by artist John S. Blunt (1798–1835), who possibly saw the launch as a boy.

Because of Folsom's lessons,
David Farragut was an avid learner
and given important tasks by the officers he served under.
"It is impossible to describe all the scenes . . .
my sojourn in the Bay of Naples
left the most vivid . . . impressions. . . .
The Emperor of Austria
and the King of Naples . . . visited our ship. . . .
I acted as interpreter to the Emperor on that occasion,"
he wrote in 1818.

And in David Farragut's life as a midshipman
there were the ships he later served aboard.
With names like *John Adams* . . .
Greyhound . . . and *Sea Gull*.
These ships would be like stars . . .
shaping a constellation of duty
like those Farragut saw in the sky on clear nights at sea.

"One of the important events of my life
was obtaining an acting lieutenancy
when but little over eighteen years of age . . .
I was now . . . with men, on an equality. . . .
When I became First Lieutenant . . .
I was really commander of the vessel."

The navy was his true home . . .
and his friends were among the crews
of the ships he served on.
When Farragut was on patrol in the Mediterranean,
he didn't know his brother George had drowned at age nine
near New Orleans . . .
or that two years later,
his father George had died of poor health.
William Farragut, still in the navy, also had a life at sea . . .
and his sisters Nancy and Elizabeth
were growing up far away in New Orleans and Pascagoula.

When Farragut came home from his ships,
he went to Green Bank.
"I was a stranger in my native land,
knowing no one but . . . Porter and his family."

THE LIEUTENANT

3

COMMISSIONED
JANUARY 13, 1825
BY PRESIDENT JAMES MONROE

1824–1840

In Norfolk, Virginia, on the Elizabeth River
and in the harbor of Portsmouth
across the water,
the US Navy had a naval station.
It was to Norfolk that David Farragut often
sailed to and from in his many sea voyages.
During shore duty, he made good friends in the port.
He liked Norfolk,
here on the eastern edge of the country he loved,
and he began to call it home.

Just before he earned the rank of lieutenant,
Farragut courted a pretty girl, four years younger,
Susan Caroline Marchant,
who had a July birthday as he did.
David Farragut was ready for his own house on land . . .
one he could return to after sea duty.

On September 2, 1824, a Thursday,
David was married in Trinity Church
to Susan . . . who was nineteen
and took his bride to visit Meridian Hill,
the new Washington estate of the Porter family.
There Farragut saw David Dixon Porter, age 11,
the boy who'd been born during his *Essex* cruise.

After returning to Norfolk
and celebrating his commission for lieutenant
signed by James Monroe . . .
such a bright day for David Glasgow Farragut . . .

the next years would unfold with much pain
for his wife Susan who became ill
with neuralgia, a disease of the nerves,
and was often too weak to walk . . .

and for Captain David Porter,
who had troubles brewing in his naval career.
On a patrol in the West Indies,
Porter had invaded a village in Puerto Rico
that had jailed a member of his crew.
This action was seen as dishonorable
and illegal by the US Navy,
so the famous captain was found guilty
in a court-martial
and suspended from duty for six months.

Feeling his disgrace was unjust,
Porter resigned from the navy in 1826 . . .
and took a job for the next three years,
as commander-in-chief of the Mexican navy.
Ships were still part of his life.

When Lieutenant Farragut sailed home
from sea duty . . .
aboard the *Ferret*, his first command,
or the *Brandywine*,
one of the fastest ships in the world,
or later, the *Alert*,
he requested shore duty in Norfolk.
His wife needed his constant care,
and he never left her side.

USS *Brandywine* was a fast new frigate built at the Washington Navy Yard. Farragut served aboard this ship as a lieutenant in 1825 when she carried the famous General Lafayette home to France after his last visit to America.

But when the navy sent him orders
to patrol in Brazil . . . or the West Indies . . .
aboard the *Constellation* or the *Erie*
Lieutenant Farragut left his wife and house on Duke Street
to serve his country . . .
a country that was growing with new cities
and states and people.
The US Navy was growing, too.
With faster ships and bigger guns and more sailors.

And David Farragut was a part of it,
sailing at sea, training younger officers,
and always,
being proud he was an American.

Then, in Norfolk, on Christmas Day in 1840,
the frail Susan Farragut began three days
of painful nerve spasms
and died on December 28.
As her husband later wrote,
"She terminated a life of unequalled suffering,
which she bore . . . for sixteen years,
setting an example, to all sufferers,
of calmness and fortitude
under the severest afflictions
that would do honor to the greatest Christians."

Portrait of Lieutenant David
Glasgow Farragut, painted in
1838 by William Swain

THE
COMMANDER

COMMISSIONED
SEPTEMBER 8, 1841
BY PRESIDENT JOHN TYLER

FALL 1841

After Susan's death,
David Glasgow Farragut reached a higher rank . . .
commander . . .
the same rank that David Porter had held
before the cruise on the *Essex*.
Farragut still wrote to his mentor
who had returned from Mexico.
Porter loved his country . . .
so he found a way to serve America in a new way—
as a US diplomat to the Barbary States
and the Ottoman Empire.

During those years,
new Commander Farragut couldn't fathom any other life
than the one that took him to sea
and then brought him home to his country.

His commission was dated September 8, 1841,
and signed by President Tyler.

Soon he would sail to Brazil
and serve on the *Delaware* as executive officer
and then on the *Decatur*.

Duty.

Always it was part of Farragut.

1843

To regain his health
after some fevers from duty at sea,
David Farragut spent the summer of 1843
sixty miles from Washington, DC,
in the mountains of Virginia at Fauquier Springs,
a town with mineral waters, a hotel,
and guest cottages.
There he met Virginia Loyall . . . from a Norfolk family.
She was the oldest of five daughters
and won his heart with her kindness,
respect for the US Navy,
and love of reading books.

At Christ Church in Norfolk
on December 26, 1843,
soon after her nineteenth birthday,
Virginia married Commander Farragut.
The Farraguts took a wedding trip to New York
and returned to Norfolk
to live aboard the *Pennsylvania* . . .
the largest of US warships.
At the Navy Yard,
she was used as a receiving ship . . . a ship to train recruits.

U. S. SHIP OF THE LINE PENNSYLVANIA, 140 Guns.

Lithograph of the USS *Pennsylvania*, 1846

1844–1855

In October of 1844,
Loyall Farragut, named after Virginia's family,
was born in Norfolk.
In their quarters on the *Pennsylvania*,
David made a tiny hammock for his infant son
to hang above his wife's bed . . .
that she could raise and lower with a pulley.

Loyall.
A healthy little sailor.

In May of 1846,
the United States went to war with Mexico.
The conflict lasted for two years . . .
and during part of it,
David Farragut was ordered by the Navy Department
to serve aboard the sloop *Saratoga*,
as part of a blockade of Mexican ports
by American ships.
After winning the war,
the US swelled with territories
that had earlier belonged to Mexico.

The year the war ended, 1848,
Commander Farragut served as second in command
at the Norfolk Navy Yard
until he was assigned to duty in Washington in 1850,
the same year California, now part of the United States,
became a state.
With the nation expanding,
the US Navy would grow with it . . .
with a shipyard on the Pacific coast . . .
to build and refit American ships.

Who
could take such a plan and put it into action?
In Washington, in 1854,
the secretary of the navy tapped David Farragut.

With new orders,
the commander and Virginia packed their trunks in Norfolk
and after an arduous journey
by land and sea,
arrived at Mare Island in San Pablo Bay
near San Francisco,
the site chosen for the shipyard.
For their first eight months there,
the Farragut family lived aboard the USS *Warren.*
Loyall, aged ten, often went with his father
to watch craftsmen build or repair boats
and saw sailors in blue salute his papa with respect.

David Farragut used his skills
to plan and design a strong naval station.
He wasn't at sea,
but he was serving his nation in an important way.

Virginia and Loyall Farragut, around 1850, with Loyall holding a sword that belonged to his grandfather George Farragut

David Farragut hired a young artist to create this drawing of Mare Island for the secretary of the navy. His note reads in part: "Sending to you a bird's eye view of this Navy Yard, showing the result of our labors since we landed on this isolated, but to me most interesting spot, as I feel that my name will for many years be associated with it for good or evil; . . . as the one who . . . faithfully (carried) out the views of the government in the establishment of the first great Arsenal and Naval Depot on the Pacific Coast of America."

Farragut had reached each rung of the navy ladder.
So many ships . . . so many travels.
He was fifty-four years old.

At Mare Island . . .
near the Pacific where he'd sailed
on the *Essex* as a boy,
the news came from Washington:
President Pierce had signed his commission for captain
on September 14, 1855.

David Glasgow Farragut had earned the highest rank.
As captain,
he would wear three stripes on his sleeve.

Ships. The sea. His country.

On that day,
he thought of David Porter,
his guardian and friend
who had died twelve years before.
He thought of Lieutenant Downes, from the *Essex*,
who had risen to the rank of captain.
Who'd commanded the naval station in Boston.
These were the officers he'd looked up to
as a boy.

And he thought of Charles Folsom, his teacher in Tunis,
who'd taught at Harvard College . . .
who still sent him letters.

And of Virginia, his great encourager.
And he thanked the god he prayed to daily in faith.

All had believed in him.

Earliest known photo of David G. Farragut, taken at Mare Island around 1854

CAPTAIN

COMMISSIONED
SEPTEMBER 14, 1855
BY **PRESIDENT FRANKLIN PIERCE**

1859-1860

On New Year's Day in 1859,
Captain Farragut began almost two years at sea
in the new age of steam.
The ship he commanded was the powerful USS *Brooklyn*.
At home with Loyall in Norfolk,
Virginia Farragut watched shadows darken the nation
her husband served.
Shadows and voices and opinions.

When Farragut left the *Brooklyn* to return to shore duty,
words and news swirled through America:
the rights of states . . .
almost four million people enslaved . . .
votes in Congress . . .
for or against . . .
states where all were free . . .
states where some were not . . .
factories and money in the North . . .
cotton and farms
worked by those in bondage in the South.

And he watched as his friends began to take sides.
In Norfolk where slavery was legal,
and in parts of the South,
there was talk of *secession* . . .
states leaving the country to make a new one.
In Washington,
there was talk of war . . . to keep all the states together.

Then,
after Abraham Lincoln from Illinois
was elected president,
seven states in the South voted to secede . . .
to leave the union of the United States,
so they could have their own Confederate States of America.

Inauguration of Mr. Lincoln, 4 March, 1861 on the East Portico of the unfinished Capitol by an unknown photographer. The inauguration of President James Buchanan in 1857 was the first to be photographed.

SPRING 1861

A month after Lincoln's inauguration on March 4,
the second to ever be photographed,
Confederate soldiers captured Fort Sumter
in Charleston's harbor . . .
the same harbor where George Farragut
had smuggled guns past the British in 1776.

When David Farragut heard the news,
his face was grim for the future of his country.

A federal fort.

The American flag taken down.

Two days later, on April 15,
Abraham Lincoln called up troops
to put down the rebellion
and keep all the states together.
On April 17,
Virginia voted to leave the Union.
Virginia . . .
David Farragut's home for forty years
when he was not on a ship at sea.

**Abraham Lincoln in Illinois
before taking office, 1861**

On April 12, 1861, the South Carolina militia fired on
Fort Sumter, a federal (Union) fort held by the US Army.

The next morning,
he heard about the vote . . .
at a store where he met for coffee with his friends.
Some had already *resigned* from the US Navy
to serve the South.
Captain Farragut walked with sadness
to his house on Duke Street
where, when not away at sea,
he'd lived for more than twenty years.

As a seven-year-old boy,
Glasgow Farragut had made a choice.
Now at age fifty-nine,
Captain David Glasgow Farragut had to choose.
Would he serve the North or the South?

He'd been *born* in the South.
And his wife Virginia and his son Loyall
had been born in Norfolk.

He'd *lived* in New Orleans . . .
and his brother William's family was there.
His sisters Nancy and Elizabeth
had families in Louisiana and Mississippi.

But for fifty-one years,
Farragut had saluted the Stars and Stripes . . .
and served his country.
His warrant—signed G. Farragut—
was his life's compass.
He'd do whatever it took to defend the United States.
There was only one path.

Duty.

That day,
David Farragut told Virginia he would "follow the flag"
and that if she left with him,
it was uncertain when or if she would see her relatives again.
Married for almost twenty years,
Mrs. Farragut also had to choose . . .
to stand *with* her husband
and not with her family in Norfolk.

Loyall, who was sixteen,
was with his parents that afternoon
when they boarded a steamer to Baltimore
and then traveled to New York City.

After the family's departure,
in Norfolk,
some would call Farragut a traitor to the South.

Duty.

In New York,
where the Farraguts stayed for a few days,
crowds were everywhere,
talking of war, war, war.
Men were enlisting, each with his own reason.
For adventure.
Or patriotism.
Or to punish the rebel states.
Or to rid the country of slavery.
Or to defend and preserve the Union.

The family traveled on to Hastings-on-Hudson,
a town twenty miles north
where Virginia had a cousin...
and made their home at 128 Washington Avenue.
David Farragut again lived near a river...
this time, a few blocks
from the east bank of the majestic Hudson.

Duty.

During the Civil War years, the Farraguts rented half of the Draper Cottage on
Washington Avenue in Hastings-on-Hudson.

On April 19,
Lincoln signed a proclamation to blockade all southern ports.

*Whereas an Insurrection against the Government of the United
States has broken out in the States of South Carolina, Georgia,
Alabama, Florida, Mississippi, Louisiana, and Texas...*

And whereas a combination of persons . . . have threatened to . . . commit assaults on the lives, vessels, and property of good citizens of the country lawfully engaged in commerce on the high seas, and in waters of the United States . . . .

Now, therefore, I, Abraham Lincoln, President of the United States . . . have further deemed it advisable to set on foot a blockade of the ports within the States aforesaid. . . . For this purpose a competent force will be posted so as to prevent entrance and exit of vessels from the ports aforesaid. If, therefore, with a view to violate such blockade, a vessel shall approach, or shall attempt to leave either of the said ports, she will be duly warned by the commander of one of the blockading vessels, who will endorse on her register the fact and date of such warning, and if the same vessel shall again attempt to enter or leave the blockaded port, she will be captured and sent to the nearest convenient port, for such proceedings against her and her cargo as prize as may be deemed advisable.

And I hereby proclaim and declare that if any person . . . shall molest a vessel of the United States, or the persons or cargo on board of her, such person shall be held amenable to the laws of the United States for the prevention and punishment of piracy;

In witness whereof, I have hereunto set my hand, and caused the seal of the United States to be affixed.

Done at the City of Washington, this nineteenth day of April, in the year of our Lord one thousand eight hundred and sixty one, and of the Independence of the United States the eighty-fifth.

And at the Norfolk naval station on April 20,
the top officer issued his own orders:
the masts and decks of the *Pennsylvania*
were burned to the waterline by Union sailors
along with sheds, docks,
and US Navy ships in the harbor.
Smoke and sparks blew across the Elizabeth River,
whose current carried charred timbers.

Best to *destroy* the station and its ships
than let them be used
by the Confederate States of America,
the eight states that had their own army and navy . . .
and a president, a man named Jefferson Davis,
who'd served in the US Army and the US Senate
before joining the cause of the South.
Two more states . . . and then Tennessee,
would soon join the Confederacy.

Destruction of the Norfolk Navy Yard
in April 1861 from *Harper's Weekly*

President Lincoln and Genl. Scott Reviewing 3 years regiment on Penn Ave. 1861 by Alfred Waud, an English-born artist. Waud came to America in 1850 and during the Civil War worked as an artist correspondent, creating sketches in the field that were rushed to newspapers.

FALL 1861

Months later,
David Dixon Porter,
the boy born to Evelina Porter at Green Bank in 1813,
was now a naval lieutenant.
At a meeting with Gideon Welles,
the secretary of the navy
who was planning the blockade,
it was Porter who stated
that the best captain on the navy's list
to lead a fleet
was the officer he'd known since childhood:
David Glasgow Farragut.

Farragut was given orders,
the most important in his navy life . . .
to command a *fleet* . . .
the Western Gulf Blockading Squadron.

His ships were to stop trade in the South . . .
to block boats from sailing in and out of ports
from the Rio Grande River on the border with Mexico
to St. Andrew Bay in Florida.

And . . .
President Lincoln wanted him to capture
the biggest port of the Confederacy . . .

New Orleans.

WINTER 1862

Farragut's flagship was the *Hartford*.

A steam sloop, much like the *Brooklyn*,
of two hundred and twenty-five feet,
she carried three masts with sails . . .
two engines . . .
guns . . .
and cannon.

Gilt eagle wings, carved from wood, framed her name.

On the mizzen flew a square blue flag . . .
to signal this was the fleet commander's ship.

In January of 1862
Flag Officer Farragut boarded his ship
in Philadelphia . . .
and the *Hartford* pushed through ice
on the Delaware River . . .
stopping a few miles south at Fort Mifflin . . .
where Confederate prisoners-of-war
would be held . . .
to load powder and shells onto the gun decks.

Then on downriver past the town of Chester
and Green Bank
where the fleet captain had signed his warrant.
David Farragut had just made another promise
to the navy . . .
that his ships would take New Orleans.

"As to being prepared for defeat,
I certainly am not.
Any man who is prepared for defeat
would be half defeated before he commenced.
I hope for success;
shall do all in my power to secure it,
and trust to God for the rest,"
the determined Farragut wrote during the war.

Painting of USS *Hartford* by unknown artist,
initialed F.M., about 1891

By February 20,
the *Hartford* sailed past Pensacola, Florida . . .
then Pascagoula, Mississippi,
where his sister Nancy Farragut . . .
whom Virginia and Loyall had visited before the war began . . .
lived as a widow
after the death of her husband, Louis Gurlie.
And on to Ship Island in the Gulf . . .
the landmark Captain Farragut had known as a boy.
These gleams of his boyhood . . .
New Orleans . . .
Chester . . .
Pascagoula . . .
the Mississippi Sound . . .
stirred his heart with memories.

Ship Island now had a brick fort, held by the Union.

Farragut had chosen his fleet of seventeen ships
and they began to arrive and anchor
in the deepwater bay,
a hundred miles from the mouth of the Mississippi.
"The island is a low stretch of sand,
almost as white as snow,
with no . . . vegetation except something
which looks like pine underwood,"
a Union army captain, John DeForest,
serving at the fort,
wrote to his family that March.

David Farragut's letters to the Navy Department
had this simple address:

Flag-officer D. G. Farragut, U.S. Navy
Commanding Western Gulf Blockading Squadron,
Ship Island

And in them
Farragut asked for more bandages and medicine
for his fleet's doctors
and more coal to power his ships.

The harbor at Ship Island was crowded with gunboats,
schooners,
and sloops of war.
It was the biggest force
to sail under an American flag.

SPRING 1862

As his fleet headed for the passes
that led from the salty gulf into the Mississippi,
Captain Farragut checked his maps
and met with his staff.
Each night,
he pondered the attack on New Orleans.

He'd carried a simple but deep faith across oceans.
He'd prayed at his church in Norfolk
and on the decks of many ships.
David Farragut again put his trust in God . . .
whom he called *the ruler of all things* . . .
to help him capture the port he'd known as a Tennessee boy . . .
and to raise the US flag once again
over the city square.

But, even with faith,
Farragut knew he faced hurdles.
During the winter,
mud had washed down the river
and made a bar under the water . . . like a sandbar.
The passage into the Mississippi
was too shallow for ships with deep keels.
Some would have to be *towed*
or *pushed* over the mud bar.

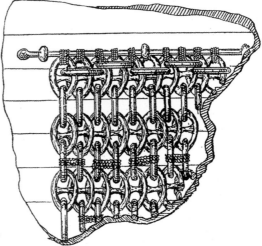

Example of chain armor used to protect ships in Farragut's fleet in April 1862

Time was slipping by.
Find ropes. Lighten loads.
And hurry.

Over the next weeks,
one by one,
his ships crossed the mud bar.
Then Captain Farragut gave orders to each crew
to circle the engines with bags of sand, ashes,
and canvas hammocks . . .
and to hang nets of chains over the wood hulls
and two feet below the waterline.
His ships now wore armor.

The prize of New Orleans,
where his mother had been buried fifty-four years before,
lay north.

Farragut double-checked his charts.
And by April 16,
at the Head of Passes in the Mississippi River,
his Union ships swung on their anchor lines . . .
waiting.

Twenty-five miles upriver on each side of the Mississippi,
two brick forts stood as sentries.
Jackson was on the western bank,
and on the eastern bank, St. Philip.

Blocking the river
was a Confederate wall of metal cables . . .
linked across the hulks of sunken ships.

After a passing French boat
signaled to the *Hartford* about the forts
You will find them very strong . . .
David Farragut told his signal officer to raise his flags:
I shall take them by audacity.
By a bold risk.

And Farragut had a steady friend to help him:
David Dixon Porter.

Porter, of lower rank,
took his orders from Farragut,
and the navy had given him a fleet of twenty sailing schooners
with a *mortar* on each . . .
to shoot bombs into the air against the enemy.

Captain Farragut hoped Porter would batter
the forts into surrender,
but the brick walls were high . . .
and the shells fired from the mortars might fall short.

David Dixon Porter (1813–1891), whose father had served as Farragut's childhood guardian, became an admiral in 1870, the second to be named an admiral in the US Navy. This photo was taken during the Civil War.

The Mortar Fleet in Trim with trees tied to masts, commanded by David Dixon Porter

To blend in with the wooded shore,
the sailors on the mortar boats
tied leafy trees on each mast . . .
and while Farragut waited on the *Hartford*,
Porter's forest flotilla moved up the river.

On April 18,
the barrage of fire from his ships began.
Boom! Crash! Boom!

For three days and nights
a storm of shells, shot, and spark
from the attacking boats and from the forts' defenders
rent the river air.
But most of the more than seven thousand bombs
from the Union side fell short . . .
and the tree branches were soon torn from the masts
by enemy fire.

The rebels sped the news upriver
to New Orleans
that Fort Jackson and Fort St. Philip still held.
Her citizens cheered
and hung Confederate flags from their windows.
Their city was *safe* now
from Farragut and the US Navy.

But Farragut was a man of valor.
And as flag officer,
he believed in his warships and in his sailors.
Quickly he gathered his captains.
They must act *now* . . .
The fleet would sail past the forts
under the cover of night.
And then on up the river . . .
to capture the prize.

Farragut ordered his crews to smear Mississippi mud
on the hulls of their boats
to darken them.
And asked his trusted fleet captain, Henry Bell,
to take two gunboats, the *Pinola* and the *Itasca*,
and steam into the channel between the forts after midnight.

As Farragut paced in the darkness of the night of April 20,
awaiting news,
his gunboats, under heavy fire by the forts,
rammed the chain that blocked the Mississippi
and snapped it in half.

A gap was made . . .
wide enough for the Union ships to pass through.
The next day,
Farragut wrote these words in a letter to a friend:
"Captain Bell went last night to cut the chain across the river.
I never felt such anxiety in my life
as I did until his return. . . .
I was as glad to see Bell . . .
as if he had been my boy.
I was up all night,
and could not sleep until he got back to the ship."

On April 23,
Farragut made a visit to each of his seventeen ships
to encourage his men and review the plan.

His four thousand sailors were ready.
They'd heard the guns of the forts
rain their fury on the mortar boats.
But they trusted this captain with the warm smile
who treated each as an equal.

The USS *Itasca* (third from left) named for the Minnesota lake near the
headwaters of the Mississippi River is pictured with gunboats quickly built for
the US Navy during the Civil War.

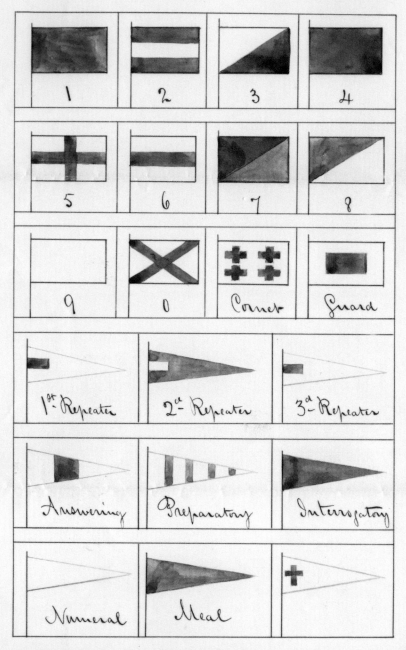

List of Farragut's signal flags, dated April 16, 1862

That same day,
General Duncan,
the Confederate commander of Fort Jackson, wrote:
"God is certainly protecting us.
We are cheerful,
and have an abiding confidence in our ultimate success."

In the evening,
Farragut stood on the deck of the *Hartford*
with his clerk who spied a lone bald eagle,
used as the symbol of America's freedom since 1782 . . .
and took it as a sign of good luck,
as the bird soared above the cluster of Union ships,
turning its powerful wings . . .
because Farragut knew the two forts would be on alert . . .
waiting for his attack.

The minutes ticked by
and an hour past midnight, now April 24,
sailors were called in whispers from their hammocks.
Silent prayers were lifted to God.

Captain Farragut checked his watch
and at 1:55 a.m. gave orders for his signal
to pull up anchors and move into position . . .
seventeen Union ships with proud crews and proud names . . .
like the *Brooklyn* . . . the *Iroquois* . . .
the *Kennebec* . . . and the *Pensacola*.
All chosen by David G. Farragut.

Two lanterns of red light soon shone
from the mizzen mast of the *Hartford*.
With noises muffled across their decks,
his ships . . .
some too slowly for Farragut . . .
took their places in two lines.

On the right was the First Division . . .
led by the gunboat *Cayuga*
that would fire to starboard at Fort St. Philip.
On the left was the Center Division
led by the *Hartford* . . .
that would fire to port at Fort Jackson . . .
and the Third Division followed behind both columns
as support.

Each ship flew a special pennant . . .
red for the First Division,
blue for the Center Division,
and red and white for the Third Division

"The enemy's lights,
while they discovered us to them,
were, at the same time, guides to us,"
Farragut later wrote.
On the ships came,
their wakes churning the Mississippi water white.
As the first ones pushed through the gap,
the rebel guns opened fire.
And Farragut's fleet returned the hail of death.

"It was as if the artillery of heaven were playing upon earth,"
Captain Farragut wrote.

At 3:55 a.m.,
the *Hartford* steamed through the open chains.
Bradley Osbon, Farragut's signal officer,
moved by the courage of Farragut and the Union ships,
raised the *Hartford*'s blue flag
and a huge Stars and Stripes.
"If we were to go down
it would be well to have our colors flying
above the water," Signal Officer Osbon later said.

Soon other ships raised their Stars and Stripes too.

A sliver of moon gleamed in the sky
and as smoke billowed across the river,
gunners on the walls of Fort Jackson
spied the big flag on the *Hartford* and took aim.
Their shells tore through the night.
For a better view of the fort,
David Farragut climbed the port side of the mizzen
with the quickness of a boy
and braced himself in the rigging.

Using a pair of opera glasses that belonged to Osbon,
Farragut squinted at the unfolding battle
and watched his fleet run the gauntlet of fire
from the two forts.

Shards of metal and splinters of wood
showered the *Hartford*,
and sailors below begged their captain to return to the deck.
Minutes after Farragut climbed down,
an enemy shot tore through the same rigging.

Then, from the shore,
the Confederates set a fireboat adrift
and in the current,
it slammed against the *Hartford*.
The raft sank when Farragut's crew heaved a bomb on it.
But it was too late . . .
already a wall of flames licked across the wood decks
of the flagship.

Farragut stood in the smoke and called orders
as his firemen rushed to train hoses on the blaze.
"The ship was one blaze all along the port side,
halfway up to the main and mizzen tops,"
Lieutenant Albert Kautz, at age 23,
who was aboard the *Hartford*,
later recorded.
"The flames . . . struck terror to all hearts."

Capture of New Orleans, Farragut passing the forts by night,
painted by Julian Oliver Davidson in 1886

As the *Hartford* smoldered and shifted in a crosscurrent,
the starboard gun crews kept loading and firing
and loading and firing,
pouring shot and shells, screeching and hot . . .
in a bright cascade on Fort St. Philip.

David Farragut never stopped shouting courage
to his crew . . .
and he never lost his sense of direction
while he spoke to the helmsman guiding the ship
and checked a tiny compass on his watch chain.

The *Hartford* lunged ahead like a charred beast of war,
with amazingly
only ten sailors wounded and three dead
out of a crew of 310 men.

That night,
on this stretch of river that was half a mile wide,
fourteen of Farragut's seventeen ships
slipped through the gap in the chain barrier
and ran the hail of fire.
The battle of passing the forts
lasted ninety minutes.
Only one Union ship, the *Varuna*, was lost
when she sank in combat.
Eight of her crew would receive the Medal of Honor
for their bravery.

Then Farragut's squadron swept north up the river
en route to New Orleans . . .
to attack a rebel fleet of fifteen ships
and destroy their ram, the *Manassas*.

The Battle of New Orleans by Thomas S. Sinclair, created between 1862 and 1865, shows Farragut's fleet passing the forts.

A painting by Worden Wood (1880–1943) shows the USS *Brooklyn* engaging the Confederate ram *Manassas* on April 24, 1862. The *Manassas* was one of the first ironclad ships to be in combat.

Each Confederate vessel
was either captured or destroyed.
Now in the great port,
there were whispers of fear and anger.
Nothing must fall to Farragut's fleet.
Barges stacked high with bales of cotton
were set on fire
and pushed into the currents to glide south.

David Farragut had no words . . .
just deep sadness . . .
as his Union crews brushed the flaming bales aside
and sailed north.

With nothing left to stop them,
the fleet anchored bow to stern in a line,
their port guns aimed at the city . . .
once the beating heart of trade for all the South.
New Orleans had burned her own docks.

Farragut could only look to his god
as he watched a sudden storm
wash over his fleet and the defiant city.
A torrent of rain hissed into the harbor's fires.

The tears of a nation . . . North and South.
Sodden flags hung from the balconies of the city
where a Tennessee boy had been on the muster roll
at age eight.

David Farragut penned a quick note to Virginia:
I took the city at meridian to-day.

Farragut's fleet below New Orleans, by Dutch-born American painter
Mauritz Frederick de Haas (1832–1895)

Such vandalism I never witnessed
as the destruction of property.
All the beautiful steamers and ships
were set on fire and consumed. . . .
I have only time to thank God
and bless you both.
Give my love to the family and all the neighbors.

In victory,
the sixty-year-old Farragut issued orders
and waited on the *Hartford*
after he sent his officers ashore
to ask for the surrender of the port.
Citizens jeered the Union men
as they walked unarmed

through an angry mob.
Captain Farragut set aside an hour,
beginning at 11:00 a.m. on April 26,
for all fleet officers and crews
to return thanks to God.

On April 29,
the Confederate flag was lowered by Union hands,
aided by Lieutenant Kautz from the *Hartford*,
not by those of defiant New Orleans citizens . . .
and the Stars and Stripes flew once again
above the city hall.

The Levee at New Orleans on the afternoon of the 29 of April, 1862 with the Union Party landing to Demand the Surrender of the City is attributed to English-born William Waud (1830–1878), Alfred Waud's brother. He labeled church spires in the background.

SUMMER 1862

Newspapers in the North told the story . . .
of the two forts that surrendered
soon after Farragut's fleet passed them
and took New Orleans.

Captain David Glasgow Farragut was a hero.

His deeds of audacity were spoken of *everywhere* . . .
even across the seas.
By reporters at their desks,
farmers in their fields,
and citizens on their streets . . .
but never by the man himself.

Farragut had given Lincoln the prize the Union needed
and shown that *ships* were as important
as armies in battle.
In July,
Congress voted to create the rank of *rear admiral*
for David G. Farragut . . .
a higher rank than captain.
He was the first navy officer to earn this honor.

On August 12,
Farragut wrote to his family:
"Yesterday
I hoisted my flag at the main,
and the whole fleet cheered,
which I returned with a most dignified salute."

6

THE
REAR ADMIRAL

COMMISSIONED
JULY 16, 1862
BY **PRESIDENT ABRAHAM LINCOLN**

A rear admiral's flag carries
two white stars on a blue field.

WINTER 1863

Farragut still commanded the Western Gulf
Blockading Squadron
and his work was constant . . .
with travels to Pensacola in Florida,
to Ship Island,
to New Orleans,
and to battles up and down the Mississippi,
helping David Dixon Porter,
whose orders were to put the river under Union control.

After the prize of New Orleans was captured,
France and England,
whom the Confederate states tried to win to their side,
stayed neutral in the war.
But President Lincoln,
the Secretary of the Navy Gideon Welles,
and David Farragut
all knew the other big port on the Gulf . . . Mobile, Alabama . . .
was now the South's lifeline to the sea.

On January 31, in Washington DC,
President Lincoln signed the Emancipation Proclamation,
freeing the enslaved in all Confederate States.
Soon, more Black men would serve as soldiers
and sailors for the Union.
The battles to keep the nation as one
were now also battles for freedom.

The rear admiral asked his son Loyall
to serve as his clerk aboard the *Hartford*
writing letters and orders at the tall oak desk
in his quarters.
The son he loved so dearly was with him each day.
And each day,
Loyall saw the respect given to his father
by the officers and crew.

The river battles at Baton Rouge . . .
Natchez . . .
Vicksburg . . .
and Port Hudson . . .
and the long months of command
wore on Farragut's health.
His deepwater ships were meant for the sea,
not a river.
Nothing was won easily.

Port Hudson—which, like Vicksburg, was on high bluffs on the Mississippi River—was held by the Confederates and endured a siege until its surrender on July 9, 1863. *Rear Admiral Farragut's Fleet Engaging the Rebel Batteries at Port Hudson, March 14th, 1863* is a hand-colored lithograph by Currier & Ives, possibly created in 1863.

But the blockade from Florida to Mexico held.
On moonless nights,
fast Confederate boats slipped past the Union ships,
but not many.
In March of 1863,
Loyall left the *Hartford* to return home
to Hastings-on-Hudson.
He hoped to enter West Point, the school for army officers,
forty miles to the north . . .
or the Naval Academy, now in Newport, Rhode Island.

Watercolor of the USS *Hartford* (with a pale hull) by R.G. Skerrett, created after the Civil War

SUMMER 1863

David Farragut was often ill with chills and fevers.
He hadn't seen Virginia for a year and a half . . .
but their letters to each other, which took weeks to arrive,
were filled with devotion.

The news from the battles fought on land
brought anguish to the man
to whom *country* was everything.
His own family had been divided by loyalties.
William Farragut's sons, who'd grown up in New Orleans,
fought for the South . . .
as did Elizabeth's family in Pascagoula.
And in Pennsylvania,
less than a hundred miles from Chester,
thousands in uniform from both sides,
blue or gray,
had fought and died on July wheat fields
in a town called Gettysburg.

That August,
his flagship *Hartford* that had taken over two hundred hits
by shot and shells from New Orleans
and other battles
carried the weary rear admiral home to his family.

WINTER 1864

After a few months in Hastings-on-Hudson,
David Farragut was rested
and ready to again serve the Union . . .
with orders from Secretary Welles in Washington.

In the new year of 1864,
the *Hartford*, with repaired rigging and decks,
put to sea at Sandy Hook near New York City
as a snowstorm swirled through her masts.

The rear admiral ordered his pilot
to check the compasses and set the course . . .

south to the Gulf of Mexico.

Rear Admiral Farragut's mission:
to take Mobile Bay.
After losing New Orleans,
the Confederates had fortified this waterway to the Gulf.
The bay was their biggest link to trade
and they knew President Lincoln wanted it . . .
to help win the war.

To defend the bay,
the Confederate navy built water barriers,
and they had a brand-new ironclad ram.

She was almost as long as the *Hartford*
with metal plates across her wide beam . . .
six big guns . . .
a crew of 133 men . . .
and a beak on her bow for ramming ships.

Her speed was slow, only six miles per hour . . .
but she was the most powerful ship in the Confederacy.

Her name: the *Tennessee*.

The Confederate ram *Tennessee* was painted by F. Muller around 1900.

SPRING 1864

Islands, sandbars, and three forts . . .
Morgan, Gaines, and Powell . . .
laced the entrance to Mobile Bay.

David Farragut knew from reports and rebel deserters
that the channel
between Fort Morgan and Fort Gaines
had three lines of underwater mines,
anchored by chains.
The mines were called *torpedoes* . . .
and when hit,
would explode under a ship.

And Farragut knew
a path of water *without* any hidden torpedoes
was east of a black buoy . . .
but above it,
watchful gunners of Fort Morgan could rake his ships.
Another danger:
in the shallows between Fort Gaines and the torpedoes
stood a wall of four rows of wood posts.

Thirty miles to the north of all these traps
was Mobile . . . at the top of the bay.

David Farragut's mission was to own those waters.
"We must take the world as it comes,"
he wrote to Loyall in early April.

His goal was to capture the *bay*
and let the *city* of Mobile be taken by the Union army.
"I must confess I don't like to work
in seven and nine feet of water,
and there is no more
within several miles of Mobile.
The enemy has barricaded the channel
with forts, piles, and sunken vessels."

Farragut asked the navy to send him ships
called *monitors* ...
good in shallow water.
Monitors were slower than wooden ships ...
but had metal sides and decks.
He'd need them to battle the *Tennessee*.

This photo of Franklin Buchanan was taken by one of America's earliest photographers, Mathew Brady. Buchanan was born in Baltimore and was a year older than David Farragut. He served in the US Navy after being appointed a midshipman in 1815. The first superintendent of the Naval Academy in Annapolis, he commanded the Washington Navy Yard until the start of the Civil War when he resigned from the US Navy to side with the Confederate States. In August 1862, the Confederacy gave him the rank of admiral.

And David Farragut knew his enemy... Franklin Buchanan.
From Maryland,
he'd served in the US Navy for forty-five years
and had been the first superintendent
of the US Naval Academy in Annapolis,
then joined the rebel side early in the war.
Buchanan had been named an *admiral* by the Confederates,
the only naval officer to hold this highest rank...
and the *Tennessee* was his flagship.

Mathew Brady photographed David Farragut around 1863.

SUMMER 1864

Out in the Gulf on the *Hartford*,
Farragut waited for the monitors to arrive . . .
the *Tecumseh*, the *Manhattan*, the *Winnebago*,
and the *Chickasaw* . . .
and also soldiers in blue,
under Union Major General Gordon Granger
who would attack Fort Gaines from the land side.

David wrote a letter to Virginia on July 6,
a day after his sixty-third birthday . . .
and told her he was feeling old . . .
weary from the war
that had torn apart families and the country.

This was the year David Farragut gave up
his handspring on deck.
His energy must go to taking Mobile Bay.

Farragut called his fleet captains to his quarters.

Across a table,
he'd placed little blocks of wood,
carved by the *Hartford*'s carpenter
in the shape of ships.
He moved the blocks back and forth . . .
to check speeds for each ship
and plan the best attack.

Each captain hoped for a breeze from the southwest . . .
to blow the battle smoke *toward* Fort Morgan
and make it hard for enemy gunners to see.
And the Union fleet must sail on a flood tide . . .
when the ocean current was flowing in,
not ebbing out.
Farragut knew if any ships
were put out of action in battle,
a flood tide would carry them into the bay.

Each of his warships would advance
with a smaller ship tied to its side with ropes and cables.

The pairs would sail in a line
into the clear channel under the guns of Fort Morgan . . .
and stay to the *east* of the black buoy
that marked the mined waters.

The torpedo field was west of the buoy.

Farragut wanted to lead the fleet in the *Hartford* . . .
with the *Metacomet*,
a side-wheeler named for a Wampanoag war chief,
lashed to its side.
But he agreed to be second in line behind the *Brooklyn*
when his staff warned him
his flagship would be a sure target . . .
the attack might fail if the *Hartford* was knocked out of action
or worse, sunk, early in the battle.

This photo of artwork by Xanthus Smith (1839–1929) shows the USS *Metacomet* at Pensacola, Florida, after the Battle of Mobile Bay.

In mid-July,
Farragut gave an order
to take down rigging and topmasts.
Once again,
bags of sand circled engines and guns.
And a mesh armor of chains covered each hull.

By the first of August,
heat shimmered across Mobile Bay.
Mosquitoes swarmed in the Confederate forts
and across the Union ships, two miles out to sea.

Each side waited to clash:
the three lines of gunners at Fort Morgan . . .
the soldiers bagging sand at Fort Gaines . . .
the sailors on the Confederate gunboats
near Fort Morgan, safe in its shadow.

And the crews on David Farragut's ships
near Sand Island
at the entrance to the bay.
In the engine rooms of three of his Union monitors . . .
and inside Confederate Admiral Buchanan's turtle of a ship,
the *Tennessee* . . .
men became faint
in heat that rose to over one hundred degrees.

Thousands of sailors and soldiers . . .
waiting in the August heat
and willing to die for their side . . .

North . . . or South.

On August 4,
Rear Admiral Farragut wrote a letter to Virginia:

Flagship Hartford
Western Gulf Blockading Squadron.
Off Mobile, August 4, 1864

My dearest Wife,
I write and leave this letter for you.
I am going into Mobile
Bay in the morning if
"God is my leader" as I
hope he is, and in him
I place my trust, if
he thinks it is the proper
place for me to die
I am ready to submit
to his will, in that as
all other things. . . .
The Tecumseh has not
yet arrived from Pensacola.
God bless and preserve you
my darling and my dear
boy, if anything should
happen to me — and may
his blessings also rest upon
your dear mother and
all your sisters and their
children.

Your devoted and affectionate husband,
who never
for one moment forgot
his love, duty, or fidelity –
to you his devoted and
best of wives.

D. G. Farragut

A fourth monitor, the *Tecumseh* . . .
named for a Shawnee war chief . . .
arrived at dusk in time to join the attack
the next morning.
Farragut drew a final sketch of his plan
and signed his name.
Copies were given to his captains.

In a rare picture, the USS *Tecumseh* (middle) heads to join the fleet at Mobile Bay.
It was painted by the captain's clerk, Xanthus Smith, aboard the USS *Augusta* (right).

Diagram to supersede the previous one.

Brooklyn and Octorara	00	0	Tecumseh
Hartford & Metacomet	00	0	Manhattan
Richmond and Port Royal	00	0	Winnebago
Lackawanna & Seminole	00	0	Chickasaw
Monongahela & Kennebec	00		
Ossippee and Itasca	00		
Oneida and Galena.	00		

Flag Ship Hartford. Aug 4. 1864

The above order diagram will be observed in forming line of Battle tomorrow morning or whenever the Fleet goes in.

D. G. Farragut
Rear Admiral.

[AE 1748]

Rear Admiral Farragut's hand-drawn sketch of his battle plan for Mobile Bay

Their ships would fight their way
past Fort Morgan into Mobile Bay
and then destroy the *Tennessee* . . .
or be destroyed by the fort's guns and the monster ram.
"It was the confidence reposed in him . . .
and his . . . faith in the success . . .
that inspired all around him,"
one of his officers later said.

At three in the morning on Friday, August 5,
Rear Admiral Farragut awoke . . .
and asked his steward, John Brooks,
to check the weather.
It was hot but the breeze was from the southwest . . .
a good sign.

At the same time,
a sailor aboard the *Manhattan*
saw a comet flash across the sky . . .
and recorded this in the monitor's log.

Harbor and River Monitor USS *Manhattan*, commissioned on June 6, 1864

Pipes sounded and drums rolled . . .
calling sailors to their stations.
Each had a job to do.
And every man was important.

The water shone in the dawn light
with a few ripples.
Then the ships took their places.
The four monitors, led by the *Tecumseh*,
were waiting near Sand Island.
They would cross in front of the line
to trade the first fire with Fort Morgan.

The *Brooklyn*, with the smaller *Octorara* by her side,
was in the lead of the wooden ships.

And behind them,
the *Hartford* with the *Metacomet*.

At 6:00 a.m.,
all were sailing on the flood tide toward Mobile Bay.

When the sun rose forty minutes later,
American flags were flying from masts on every ship . . .
and Farragut's blue flag fluttered from the mizzen
of the *Hartford*.

Soon the four monitors were fired on by Fort Morgan . . .
and their Union guns boomed back.

By 6:45 a.m., the *Hartford*'s guns began.

Even with the southwest breeze,
smoke drifted across her deck
and Farragut, telescope in his hand,
climbed into the port rigging step by step . . .
and stood against a mast to get a better view
of the dangerous channel.
Worried for the rear admiral's safety,
John Knowles, an officer on deck,
climbed up with a line
and insisted on looping it around Farragut
to keep him safer.
One of the pilots of the *Hartford*,
Martin Freeman,
was in the rigging of another mast . . .
and on the *Metacomet*,
Lieutenant Commander James Jouett stood atop
the wheelhouse.
All three men could now see the Union fleet
above the smoke and din.

Then the *Tecumseh*, the best of the four monitors,
veered off course.
Instead of going *east* of the black buoy . . .
she sailed *west* and hit a mine.
Farragut and sailors on other ships watched in horror
as the *Tecumseh* tilted to port and sank bow first . . .
her propeller on the stern,
spinning in the air.
The monitor,
with a crew of 114 men trapped inside,
sank in five quick minutes
as bubbles swirled in the calm water.

Only twenty-one sailors would swim free.

During these minutes of shock,
the three other monitors slowed down.
And the *Brooklyn* and *Octorara*,
steaming toward them,
stopped to avoid collision . . .
and then tried to back up
as the guns from Fort Morgan
raked the Union ships.

To avoid disaster,
Farragut told his signal flag officer
to send a message to the *Brooklyn*.

Go on.

But the monitors were now out of position.

David Farragut called upon God
with a silent prayer.
An instant later,
he told his officers to go forward
and sail *past* the *Brooklyn*.
His flagship must seize the moment
and lead the line.
And the torpedoes?
The *Tecumseh* was lost . . .
but Farragut hoped the mines would be faulty
with damp gunpowder.

This image is titled *Destruction of the Monitor 'Tecumseh' by a Rebel Torpedo, in Mobile Bay, August 5, 1864*. The sunken *Tecumseh* remains in a depth of thirty feet about three hundred yards northwest of Fort Morgan and is considered a war grave. The ironclad ship is under the protection of the US Navy, pending preservation efforts.

All his life,
he'd faced choices
and trusted in his own courage.
With audacity and with valor,
Farragut called orders
to the *Hartford* and *Metacomet:*

DAMN THE TORPEDOES! FOUR BELLS!
FULL SPEED AHEAD!

Tied together,
the two ships surged forward past the *Brooklyn*
into the channel of torpedoes.

Sailors heard the mines in their round cases,
hitting the bottom of their ships . . .
Knock . . . Knock . . .
but none exploded.
Pair by pair,
the Union ships stayed in line led by the *Hartford.*

Crash! Boom!

The guns of Fort Morgan roared on.
The cries of sailors echoed on the decks
as wood splinters, ten feet long,
tore into the crews.

Hand-colored woodcut of barrel torpedoes, or mines, used by Confederates, 1860s

On the *Hartford*,
two squads of gunners were killed . . .
along with other shipmates
who were blown into the water to drown . . .
or who lay like twisted ragdolls
on the decks.

Then . . . the Union line was past the barrage of fire!
And sailing into Mobile Bay.

Battle of Mobile Bay, painted by Julian O. Davidson (1853–1894) and published by Louis Prang, shows the sinking of the USS *Tecumseh*.

Farragut climbed down from the mast
as his fleet, with a chorus of cheers,
gathered near the *Hartford*.
The rear admiral quickly gave new orders,
signal flags were flying,
and sailors rushed to their battle stations.
Now inside the bay,
Farragut's fleet would attack the big ram.
And hoping he could sink some Union ships
Admiral Buchanan and his *Tennessee*
sailed toward them.

Guns screeched and boomed.
Ships set their sails and tacked to join the fight.

One by one,
the Union monitors charged the powerful ram.
Shells bounced off her metal hull
and smoke filled the air.

Slowly,
in a cascade of fire,
the Union ships did their work . . .
as the *Tennessee* blasted back
at the monitors and wooden ships.

When the *Hartford* charged the ram,
Farragut again nimbly climbed into the port rigging
to view the position of his ships
and the Confederate fleet.

After an hour of battle,
guns on the *Tennessee* jammed,
and her steering no longer worked.
Her smokestack was almost cut in half
and Franklin Buchanan, Farragut's opposing admiral,
lay wounded.
He turned his battered flagship over to
Commander James Johnston,
who soon saw that his crew would die
if he didn't surrender.

David Farragut stands in the rigging of the USS *Hartford* during the Battle of Mobile Bay, August 5, 1864. *An August Morning with Farragut* was painted by William H. Overend in 1883.

At 10:00 a.m.,
a sailor lowered the Confederate flag
and raised a white one to give up the fearsome ram.
The next day,
soldiers at Fort Powell retreated,
blowing up the fort as they left the island.
The American flag was raised
and within days,
Fort Gaines *and* Fort Morgan surrendered.

The Union side now held Mobile Bay.

Farragut knew thousands of soldiers,
not sailors,
would be needed to capture and hold the city.
But the bay and its channel to the gulf
had been taken.
No more cotton or guns or food for the Confederacy
could pass in and out of Mobile.

Admiral Buchanan was a prisoner of war
and the Union would repair his *Tennessee*
and use her in their blockade . . .
against the side that had built her.
David Glasgow Farragut
became an even greater hero to the North.
But always,
he let others tell the stories of his deeds.

His praise was for the men he commanded . . .
sailors in blue . . .
who served in the United States Navy.

On the day of his great victory,
August 5, 1864 . . .
Farragut wept on the deck of his flagship . . .
as he stood by the row of those who gave their lives
to take Mobile Bay.
Ninety-eight men in his fleet
would earn the Medal of Honor
for their brave acts . . .
one was a coal heaver aboard the *Hartford*
who lost both arms
to help his mates during the battle.

Richard D. Dunphy, an immigrant from Ireland, was a coal heaver aboard the USS *Hartford* and was wounded during the Battle of Mobile Bay, losing both of his arms. Dunphy was awarded the Congressional Medal of Honor. This photo was taken by Samuel Masury in the 1860s. Ninety-eight Union sailors and marines received the Medal of Honor during the Battle of Mobile Bay. Fourteen were Irish immigrants.

John H. Lawson, a free Black man from Philadelphia, served as a landsman (a rank given to new recruits with little or no sea experience) aboard the USS *Hartford* at Mobile Bay. He was one of six men stationed at the shell whip on the berth deck when an enemy shell wounded or killed all six. Lawson was wounded in the leg and thrown against the side of the ship. But he refused to go below and returned to the shell whip to remain at his post during the action. He was awarded the Congressional Medal of Honor.

The terrible war wasn't over,
but the rear admiral wanted only to see Virginia and Loyall
and rest on his porch in Hastings-on-Hudson.
And so he went home
aboard the *Hartford* to New York . . .
rather than lead other sea battles for the Union.
David Farragut's health was fragile . . .
the hard years at sea had taken a toll.

Again,
his deeds were reported around the world.
The name Farragut meant victory.
And ships.
And audacity.

It meant the United States Navy.

This photograph shows David G. Farragut (far left) and his fleet captain and friend, Percival Drayton (middle), along with several other officers aboard the USS *Hartford*. David Farragut saw his beloved US Navy grow from sails to ironclad ships powered by steam.

THE
VICE ADMIRAL

COMMISSIONED
DECEMBER 21, 1864
BY PRESIDENT ABRAHAM LINCOLN

7

A vice admiral's blue flag,
with three stars on a blue field

WINTER 1864–1865

Just before Christmas,
Congress created the new rank of *vice admiral*.
The next day,
President Lincoln signed the bill
and named David G. Farragut as the country's first.

That winter,
Vice Admiral Farragut and Virginia
were guests at the opera in Washington.
hosted by President Lincoln and his wife.
Lincoln was the thirteenth president Farragut had served . . .
both had grown up on the frontier
of a new country.
And both, in different ways,
hoped for one nation . . . at peace.

The date this photograph of Virginia Farragut was taken is unknown.

This list of honorary pallbearers for President Lincoln's funeral shows Farragut's name. The vice admiral wore a badge of mourning on his sleeve and on the hilt of his sword.

A few months later,
the war that split the nation David Farragut so loved
was finally over.
But the news of peace was soon clouded . . .
by the death of Abraham Lincoln,
Farragut's commander-in-chief.
Along with Ulysses S. Grant,
the top general and hero of the North's army,
Farragut walked as a pallbearer
at the somber funeral in Washington.
He walked for *all* who served in America's navy . . .
from carpenter to gunner to vice admiral.

AMERICA'S
ADMIRAL

COMMISSIONED
JULY 25, 1866
BY **PRESIDENT ANDREW JOHNSON**

An admiral's flag with four stars

1866–1867

Months later,
Congress again created a rank for the US Navy ... the highest.

Admiral.

The date was July 25, 1866.

Admiral.

And again,
the first officer named for this rank was Farragut.
He was sixty-five years old.
Five years before, at the start of the Civil War,
the US Navy had *ninety* ships in its entire fleet ...
with only half ready for battle.
By 1865,
after building new vessels
and buying and arming merchant boats,
the navy had grown to over *six hundred* ships.
The boy who'd signed his warrant at age nine
now held the highest rank as America's *first* admiral ...

in the largest navy in the world.

A year later,
Admiral Farragut was asked to command
his navy's European squadron ...
and visit foreign harbors.
Other nations knew of America's naval power.
Farragut would sail in goodwill and peace ...
and represent the United States as a friend.

In New York,
where David and Virginia now lived on East 36th Street
in a house given to them as a gift by the city,
President Andrew Johnson attended a reception
to wish his admiral well ...
and the next day,
sent a telegram giving Virginia permission
to travel across the Atlantic with her husband.

The *Franklin* was the admiral's flagship ...
and carried thirty-nine guns
and a crew of seven hundred and fifty men.
The blue flag that flew from a mast
had *four* white stars on it.
It was the first admiral's flag
to fly above an American warship.

The USS *Franklin* was built in Kittery, Maine, at the Portsmouth Naval Shipyard, the oldest continuously operating shipyard of the US Navy. Parts of the *Franklin*, which was launched in 1864, were salvaged from the previous USS *Franklin* of 1815. From 1867–1871, she served as the flagship for the European Squadron.

In New York harbor,
thousands on the docks and on ships
cheered farewell
on the day the *Franklin* set sail.
Waving from a tugboat
was teacher and librarian Charles Folsom,
a grandfather . . .
who fifty years before
had been aboard the *Washington*
and taught his student Glasgow Farragut
when he was a midshipman in Tunis.

Chaplain Folsom had known *then*
that Glasgow's future would be remarkable.
And indeed,
the boy David Porter had set on his naval path
and that he, as a teacher,
had led to books and curiosity about the world
had given his valor and his fidelity to his country.

Across Europe,
Admiral Farragut met kings and queens and emperors.
With his kindness and grace,
he was a fine ambassador for all Americans.
There were grand celebrations
wherever the *Franklin* anchored.

Especially in Ciutadella on sunny Minorca.

Ciutadella!

The port where his father had been born.
The port Farragut had never visited.

When David and Virginia arrived on the island,
Minorcans of all ages lined the road
to cheer their famous visitor . . .
and in the old church
where Jordi Ferragut Mesquida
had been baptized in 1755,
America's first admiral prayed to his god,
the ruler of all things, with a grateful heart.

That day,
David Glasgow Farragut,
from a family of Spanish sailors,
was named a citizen of Ciutadella,
whose harbor he'd pictured in his mind
as a boy in Tennessee.

After more than a year at sea,
of sights and salutes and honors,
the *Franklin* arrived back in New York.
Farragut's health was in decline . . .
he'd given all his strength to the US Navy.

In the summer of 1870,
six years after he sailed into Mobile Bay . . .
Admiral Farragut was still on active duty
and visiting Portsmouth, New Hampshire.
At the naval yard,
he stepped onto the deck of the *Dale* . . .
an old sailing sloop built in Philadelphia,
not far from Green Bank on the Delaware River.
The admiral told a sailor
it would be the last ship of war
he'd feel beneath his feet.

Soon after this,
Farragut was too ill to leave his bed.

The USS *Dale* was built at the Philadelphia Naval Yard and
commissioned in 1839. Early in her service in the US Navy, the
Dale sailed to the Pacific and was based in Valparaiso, where
Farragut had been aboard the *Essex* as a boy.

With his beloved Virginia and Loyall at his side . . .
and a few friends and officers . . .
at noon on August 14, or at the *meridian*,
meridian!
as the admiral called that time of day
when aboard a ship,
his heart stopped beating.

And like the bright comet
that had flashed across the sky over Mobile Bay
on the eve of his great victory,

Farragut was gone.

Loyall Farragut, who served in the US Army artillery for three years, is pictured here in his West Point cadet uniform, Twenty-First Infantry Division, June of 1868.

Admiral David Glasgow Farragut, Virginia Loyall Farragut, and Loyall Farragut (left to right).

Portrait of David Farragut, by S. Jerome Uhl, painted in 1891

David Farragut's signature from the frontispiece of the book *Our Admiral's Flag Abroad*, written by James Montgomery, of the admiral's staff

ADMIRAL FARRAGUT'S LIFE STORY

ɞ When Glasgow left New Orleans with the Porters on the *Vesuvius* in 1810, it was the last time he saw his father or younger brother.

ɞ In 1815, young George drowned at the age of nine while being towed in a boat by a schooner near New Orleans. His father George, worn down by age, illness, and sadness, died in 1817 while Glasgow was on patrol in the Mediterranean.

ɞ In 1824, Farragut had his first command: the schooner *Ferret*. That year, ill with fever, he sailed aboard the *Hamlet* to New Orleans to see his sister Nancy. This ship was carrying bricks to build the same Fort Jackson that Farragut's ships later bombarded during the Civil War.

ɞ In 1825, Farragut was on the *Brandywine*, a frigate that sailed from the Potomac River to Le Havre, France . . . with a special passenger aboard: General Lafayette, a hero of the American Revolution.

ɞ William A. C. Farragut served in the navy for fifty years until his death in New Orleans just before the Civil War began. Ill health prevented him from earning ranks above lieutenant. During the Civil War, William's two sons fought for the South. As did his two sons-in-law. His sister, Elizabeth Farragut, married Celestin Dupont in 1824, lived in Pascagoula, and had a family. She died in 1886. Nancy Farragut, Glasgow and William's other sister, married Louis Gurlie (also spelled Gourlie) and lived in New Orleans and Pascagoula.

ɞ Albert Kautz, the young officer who served aboard the *Hartford* during Farragut's passing of the forts and capture

HARPER'S WEEKLY.

JOURNAL OF CIVILIZATION.

VOL. XIV.—No. 720.]   NEW YORK, SATURDAY, OCTOBER 15, 1870.   [SINGLE COPIES, TEN CENTS.
$4.00 PER YEAR IN ADVANCE.

Entered according to Act of Congress, in the Year 1870, by Harper & Brothers, in the Office of the Librarian of Congress, at Washington.

THE FARRAGUT OBSEQUIES—THE FUNERAL PROCESSION PASSING UP BROADWAY.—Sketched by Theo. R. Davis.—[See Page 659.]

of New Orleans and who is quoted in *Full Speed Ahead!*, was born in Georgetown, Ohio, not far from Point Pleasant on the Ohio River, the birthplace of the Union general Ulysses S. Grant, who became the eighteenth president of the United States. Albert Kautz was one of Farragut's officers who assisted in raising the American flag over the city hall in New Orleans in April 1862. He later was a rear admiral in the US Navy.

⚓ For their courage during the Battle of Mobile Bay, 98 Union sailors in Farragut's fleet were awarded the Congressional Medal of Honor for personal valor above and beyond the call of duty. During the Civil War, this was the only medal the navy awarded.

⚓ During his sixty years of naval duty, David Glasgow Farragut served under fifteen presidents and met six: James Madison, John Tyler, Franklin Pierce, Abraham Lincoln, Andrew Johnson, and Ulysses S. Grant.

⚓ When Farragut died, more than a thousand mourners walked behind his casket in Portsmouth, New Hampshire. That day, the flag was displayed at half-mast at all US navy yards and stations and at noon each navy yard fired seventeen minute-guns. Later, in New York City, his formal funeral procession stretched for two miles . . . the city's salute to the passing of a great man. Schools were closed and ten thousand sailors and soldiers marched as an honor guard, led by President Ulysses S. Grant. Farragut is buried in Woodlawn Cemetery in the Bronx, New York. Virginia Farragut and their son Loyall are also buried there.

In pouring rain, thousands of New Yorkers joined the funeral procession on Broadway to honor Admiral Farragut, the nation's hero.

⚓ In 1881, a statue was dedicated by President James Garfield in Washington, DC. Vinnie Ream Hoxie, the youngest artist as well as the first female artist ever to be hired by the US government for a commission, was the sculptor. The *Hartford*'s propellers were melted down to create the statue that still stands at Farragut Square.

> *Today we come to hail this hero, who comes from the sea, down from the shrouds of his flagship, wreathed with the smoke and glory of victory . . . to take his place as our honored compatriot, and a perpetual guardian of his country's glory.*
>
> **—PRESIDENT JAMES GARFIELD, 1881**

Farragut Square statue in Washington, DC

Vinnie Ream's marble statue of Abraham Lincoln, created when the artist was eighteen, is on view in the US Capitol. Ream—born in Wisconsin in 1847—won a competition in 1875 to create the bronze statue of Admiral Farragut. This portrait of her was painted by George Peter Alexander Healy around 1870.

ප Also in 1881, another Farragut statue was dedicated . . . created by the famous Augustus Saint-Gaudens. It was his first commission and stands in Madison Square Park in New York City.

Madison Square Park statue by Augustus Saint-Gaudens

ප In the early twentieth century, the US Navy authorized the building of a group of eight destroyer ships, known as Farragut-class ships, to honor our first admiral. These destroyers—*Farragut, Dewey, Hull, Macdonough, Worden, Dale, Monaghan*, and *Aylwin*—were completed in the 1930s, and all eight saw active service during World War II. Two of these ships, *Hull* and *Monaghan*, were lost during Typhoon Cobra in December 1944.

ප In the 1950s, the navy had a second Farragut-class group of destroyers built. These ten ships were guided-missile destroyers.

ප Over the years, five ships in the United States Navy have been named for David Farragut. The USS *Farragut* (DDG-99 in the Arleigh Burke destroyer class) is the most recent. It was built in Bath, Maine, and commissioned in 2006. During a tour of the Mediterranean in 2012, the crew visited the David Farragut Memorial on the island of Minorca.

ප Also in the twenty-first century, in Ireland, an old mooring anchor was found embedded in a harbor pier by a workman. It was from the *Essex* on which Farragut had sailed thousands of miles during his first cruise as a midshipman. After its capture, the *Essex* sailed under the flag of the British Royal Navy.

USS *Farragut* (DDG-99) is the fifth navy ship named in honor of Admiral David Farragut. Her home port is Naval Station Mayport near Jacksonville, Florida. DDG stands for Destroyer Designated Guided (commonly called a guided-missile destroyer).

The crew of USS *Farragut* (DDG-99) march in a Fourth of July parade in 2017 in Bristol, Rhode Island—the oldest independence parade in the nation.

⚓ Today if you visit the US Naval Academy in Annapolis, Maryland, you can see the gold watch given to David Farragut as a nine-year-old boy in 1810 by his guardian David Porter . . . the watch he carried for luck and for courage while serving America for decades in the US Navy.

Author Louise Borden aboard *La Dolce Vita* to Ship Island in the Mississippi Sound, 2019

A NOTE ON FINDING FARRAGUT

Over the years, I'd heard the name Farragut and passed by the statues of our first admiral in Washington, DC, and New York City. My husband Pete and I had watched navy lacrosse games played at Farragut Field at the US Naval Academy in Annapolis. But all I knew was that David G. Farragut was a famous American naval officer.

In 2016, on a road trip from Atlanta home to Cincinnati, I spotted a green highway exit sign on I-75: FARRAGUT. It was north of a bridge spanning the Tennessee River and south of Knoxville, which served as Tennessee's earliest capital before it was moved to Nashville where my mother was born.

Hmm, I wondered. I was curious if *this* was the same Farragut as the statue in Washington near a metro stop I often used when we lived in the DC area for a few years.

Indeed, it was.

I found that the town of Farragut, originally the area of Campbell's Station, an early Tennessee settlement, was a few miles from the birthplace of the famous hero. In 1980 the town was incorporated and took the name Farragut to honor its native son.

My curiosity about Farragut grew with these questions: How did a boy born in 1801 on the frontier of Tennessee (which became a state in 1796) end up joining the navy of the new United States? How did he grow to love ships and become our first admiral?

I was drawn to David Farragut's story because I love rivers and oceans . . . and have spent summers in boats and on lakes in northern Michigan. I also have a deep respect for the United States Navy. Before I was born, my uncle, Theodore T. Walker, graduated from the Naval Academy in 1941 and served aboard the USS *Albacore*, a submarine that was lost while on a war patrol during World War II. The entire crew perished. I wrote a picture book, *Across the Blue Pacific: A World War II Story*, to honor Ted Walker and his shipmates who'd given their lives for our country.

And so I embarked on a journey of research that

Sail in Annapolis, Maryland, home of the United States Naval Academy

took me from Annapolis, Maryland, to Washington, DC, to Farragut's birthplace on the Holston River to Ship Island in the Mississippi Sound to Norfolk, Virginia, and to Chester, Pennsylvania. I also visited Farragut's grave at Woodlawn Cemetery as well as museums, libraries, and other sites.

Woven into my study of Farragut's life was the fact that one of my long-ago ancestors was James Bryan, a Confederate naval officer from Baton Rouge, the town Glasgow's flatboat had floated past in 1807. James died in the battle on April 24, 1862 when Farragut's ships passed Forts Jackson and St. Philip. His death left

Construction of a fort on Ship Island was begun in 1859. After Confederates claimed it and then left the island in July 1861, the fort was named Fort Massachusetts by Union soldiers who arrived with Farragut's fleet. In 1969, Hurricane Camille cut the barrier island into two parts. Both were submerged during Hurricane Katrina in 2005. By early 2019, the US Army Corps of Engineers had rejoined the parts to make one island. Now Ship Island is a tourist destination via ferry.

his son William Bryan (my great-grandfather) fatherless at age six.

How remarkable that Admiral Farragut, whose fleet had sailed up the Mississippi to capture New Orleans, would a month later fire the *Hartford*'s guns on Baton Rouge where my great-grandfather lived as a child in wartime. How remarkable that our first admiral would become my hero in the twenty-first century . . . Farragut, a man of such integrity, whose duty was always to America and her flag.

Top: Navy recruiting poster from 1917

Bottom: Navy recruiting poster from the World War II era

BIBLIOGRAPHY

All quotations used in the book can be found in the following sources marked with an asterisk (*).

BOOKS

Caleo, Robert L. *Farragut and Family: The Making of an Elder Hero.* Bloomington, IN: Xlibris, 2015.

*Daughan, George C. *The Shining Sea: David Porter and the Epic Voyage of the U.S.S. Essex during the War of 1812.* New York: Basic Books, 2013.

Duffy, James P. *Lincoln's Admiral: The Civil War campaigns of David Farragut.* New York: Wiley, 1997.

*Farragut, Loyall. *The Life of David Glasgow Farragut: First Admiral of the United States Navy, Embodying His Journal and Letters.* New York: D. Appleton and Co., 1879.

Ferreiro, Larrie D. *Brothers at Arms: American Independence and the Men of France and Spain Who Saved It.* New York: Alfred A. Knopf, 2016.

Foster, Leila Merrell. *David Glasgow Farragut: Courageous Navy Commander.* Chicago: Children's Press, 1991.

*Friend, Jack. *West Wind, Flood Tide: The Battle of Mobile Bay.* Annapolis, MD: Naval Institute Press, 2004.

Headley, P. C. *Life and Naval Career of Vice-Admiral David Glasgoe Farragut* [!], New York: William H. Appleton, 1865.

*Hearn, Chester G. *Admiral David Dixon Porter: The Civil War Years.* Annapolis, MD: Naval Institute Press, 1996.

———. *Admiral David Glasgow Farragut: The Civil War Years.* Annapolis, MD: Naval Institute Press, 1998.

———. *The Capture of New Orleans 1862.* Baton Rouge: Louisiana State University Press, 1995.

Hickey, Donald R., ed. *The War of 1812: Writings from America's Second War of Independence.* New York: Library of America, 2013.

Homans, James E. *Our Three Admirals*. New York: James T. White & Co., 1899.

Kagan, Neil, and Stephen G. Hyslop. *Atlas of the Civil War*. Washington, DC: National Geographic Society, 2009.

Katz, Harry L., and Vincent Virga. *Civil War Sketch Book: Drawings from the Battlefront*. New York: W. W. Norton & Co., 2012.

Kilmeade, Brian, and Don Yaeger. *Thomas Jefferson and the Tripoli Pirates: The Forgotten War That Changed American History*. New York: Sentinel, 2016.

*Lewis, Charles Lee. *David Glasgow Farragut: Admiral in the Making*. Annapolis, MD: Naval Institute Press, 1941 and 2014.

*———. *David Glasgow Farragut: Our First Admiral*. Annapolis, MD: Naval Institute Press, 1943 and 2014.

Long, David F. *Nothing Too Daring: A Biography of Commodore David Porter, 1780–1843*. Annapolis, MD: Naval Institute Press, 1970.

Long, Laura. *David Farragut Boy Midshipman*. Indianapolis: Bobbs-Merrill, 1962.

Mahan, Alfred Thayer. *Admiral Farragut*. New York: Haskell House, 1968.

McPherson, James. *The War That Forged a Nation: Why the Civil War Still Matters*. New York: Oxford University Press, 2015.

Montgomery, James Eglington. *Our Admiral's Flag Abroad — The Cruise of Admiral D. G. Farragut, in the Flag-Ship Franklin*. New York: G. P. Putnam & Son, 1869.

Mottelay, Paul Fleury, ed. *The Soldier in Our Civil War: A Pictorial History of the Conflict, 1861–1865, Volumes 1 and 2*. New York: The J. H. Brown Publishing Company, 1885.

Naval Historical Foundation. *The Navy*. Washington, DC: Naval Historical Foundation, 2016.

*Porter, David. *Journal of a Cruise Made to the Pacific Ocean, Volume 1*. New York: Wiley & Halstead, 1822.

Porter, David Dixon. *The Naval History of the Civil War*. New York: Sherman Publishing Company, 1886.

Roop, Connie, and Peter Roop. *Take Command, Captain Farragut!* New York: Simon & Schuster, 2002.

Shorto, Russell. *David Farragut and the Great Naval Blockade.* Englewood Cliffs, NJ: Silver Burdett Press, 1991.

Spears, John R. *A Short History of the American Navy.* New York: Charles Scribner's Sons, 1907.

Stein, R. Conrad. *David Farragut: First Admiral of the US Navy.* A Proud Heritage: The Hispanic Library. Chanhassen, MN: The Child's World, 2005.

Symonds, Craig L. *Lincoln and His Admirals.* New York: Oxford University Press, 2008.

Toll, Ian W. *Six Frigates: The Epic History of the Founding of the US Navy.* New York: W. W. Norton & Co., 2006.

Turnbull, Archibald Douglas. *Commodore David Porter, 1780–1843.* New York: The Century Co., 1929.

United States. Naval War Records Office. *Official Records of the Union and Confederate Navies in the War of the Rebellion (Series I, Volumes 18 and 21)* Washington, DC: Government Printing Office, 1906.

VIDEOS

Civil War at Sea: The US Navy's Contributions to the Preservation of the Union. Sponsored by the Surface Navy Association on the occasion of the Civil War Sesquicentennial. R. H. Rositzke & Associates, (2010).

LETTERS, JOURNALS, AND PAPERS

*Hollandsworth, Jr., James G. "Union Soldiers on Ship Island During the Civil War." Mississippi History Now, an online publication of the Mississippi Historical Society, January 2006.

*Manuscript Division of the Library of Congress, Washington, DC
David Glasgow Farragut Papers, 1810–1869

Rare Book and Special Collections Division of the Library of Congress, Washington, DC

*Special Collections and University Archives, University of Tennessee, Knoxville, TN
David G. Farragut Papers, 1815–1964

VISITS TO MUSEUMS AND HISTORIC SITES

The Admiral Farragut Monument, Madison Square Park, New York City

Farragut's birthplace, near Farragut, TN

The Farragut Museum, Farragut, TN

Farragut Square statue, Washington, DC

Fort Gaines on Dauphin Island and Mobile Bay, AL

The Hampton Roads Naval Museum, Norfolk, VA

The Library of Congress, Washington, DC

National Portrait Gallery, Washington, DC

The Norfolk Naval Yard, Portsmouth, VA

Ship Island, MS

United States Naval Academy, Annapolis, MD

United States Naval Academy Museum, Annapolis, MD

United States Navy Memorial, Washington, DC

United States Navy Memorial Visitor Center, Washington, DC

Woodlawn Cemetery, The Bronx, NY

A NOTE ABOUT THE DESIGN

The design of chapter pages in *Full Speed Ahead!* uses flags that echo David Porter's numerical signal flags from his 1809 code book (pictured on page 37) when he commanded the US Navy's New Orleans station.

A NOTE ON THE FAMOUS PHRASE "DAMN THE TORPEDOES! FULL SPEED AHEAD!"

In *The Life of David Glasgow Farragut, First Admiral of the United States Navy*, written by Loyall Farragut and published in 1879, it is revealed that Farragut's actual words to his officers during the Battle of Mobile Bay were: "Damn the torpedoes! Four bells! Captain Drayton, go ahead! Jouett, full speed!"

After Farragut's naval victory, the phrase was shortened to "Damn the torpedoes, full speed ahead!" The words *full speed ahead* have been part of American determination and energy for more than one hundred and fifty years.

A WONDERFUL CREW

A bright sun and blue sky thank-you to those who sailed with me during my research and writing voyage for *Full Speed Ahead!*:

Pete Borden, our family's captain, who explored the Gulf Coast (Pascagoula, Mobile Bay, and Fort Morgan) and found my nautical maps of the Mississippi Sound after he attended the commissioning ceremony for the new USS *Cincinnati* (LCS-30) in Gulfport, MS; Catie and Marc Cohen, Ayars and Matt Ehret, and Ted Borden, who, from afar, cheered on my solo cruise to Ship Island; Sydney McCurdy, my steadfast crewmate, and Bob McCurdy, my ocean and tide expert in all weather; Kathi and Bob Roesler, who love boats and the waters of Lake Champlain; Cindy and Alex Curchin, lifelong sailors and mentors; the Leland Yacht Club, which has fostered a love of sailing for four generations of my family; Marfé Ferguson Delano; Polly Rea, the Meekers, the Barbees, the Biggs, and the Graces; Julia Barham, the brilliant and kind curator at the Farragut Museum in Farragut, Tennessee; Beth and Jerry Fotheringill, my true Washington, DC, anchors; Kristin Swanson, amazing librarian and my Annapolis/Chester researcher, warrant photographer, and friend; Tracie Logan, James Cheevers, and James C. (Chris) Rentfrow, PhD, Captain, US Navy at the United States Naval Academy Museum, Annapolis, Maryland; Mark T. Weber and the US Navy Memorial, Washington, DC; the United States Naval Academy; the Navy League of the United States; Captain Victor Delano, Commander Clement O'Brien, and Lieutenant Theodore T. Walker, Jr., USN; my friends in the map division of the Library of Congress; the John C. Hodges Library (Special Collections/David G. Farragut Papers) at the University of Tennessee in Knoxville, Tennessee; Robert L. Caleo; staff of the Library of Congress Main Reading Room; the Bookjoy group and Hardy relatives, wonderful friends from Manchester-by-the-Sea to Hattiesburg; Commodore Lee Ault Carter; the eight-year-old students who raised their hands during my book talks across the country; skipper Mike Greenwood and Jeanne; Mary Ann Aquadro, who showed me the dolphins of the Mississippi Sound, and her husband, Jim McNeil, captain of *La Dolce Vita*, Gulfport, Mississippi, who was at the helm when we cruised to Ship Island on a clear April afternoon; Maryann Macdonald and Ann Ingalls, who visited Admiral Farragut's grave with me at Woodlawn Cemetery, the Bronx, New York; Ashleigh Hoelscher, Gwen Keiffer-Blatt, Emily Gumpert, and Kim Swiderski, whose first graders cheered me on through my revision deadlines; Mary Kay Kroeger, Trish Marx, Irene Butter, Connie Trounstine, Barbara Libby, Johanna Hurwitz, George Ella Lyon, and Ashley Wolff, writers and artists on my life voyage; Franki Sibberson, Lisa Koch, Jill Colaw, Cris Tovani, Mary Sexton, Terri Pytlik, Ann Quinn, Leah Bohrer, and Steph Harvey, who continue to be my harbors in any storm; the kind staff at Awakenings, Harper's Station Starbucks, and Le Bon Café; my Breton crewmates: Jane Singleton Paul and Christy Adams (whose ancestor John Adams was an early advocate for America's new navy); Will Andersen and Ari Post of the Army and Navy Club; Congressional staffer Michael Rauber; Tony Edmunds /Architect of the Capital staff; Natalie Barry and the Hastings Historical Society; Samuel Cox, Rear Admiral, USN (Retired) and Naval Historian; Timothy L. Francis, PhD and Naval Historian; Peter C. Luebke and Dennis Wilson at the Naval History and Heritage Command/Washington Navy Yard; the Comey crew; Laura S. Jowdy and the Congressional Medal of Honor Society; Loren Long; Brandon Miller; Julie Woods; Leland sailors Abby, Henry, Brooks, and Caroline; and a salute of thanks to: Elizabeth Harding, my agent and friend; my lighthouses at Calkins Creek—Nicole Guven, Maura Taboubi, Suzy Krogulski, Nancy Seitz, and Kerry McManus; the talented designer Carol Bobolts and the team at Red Herring Design; and Carolyn Yoder, my editor and literary captain of Farragut integrity and valor who sailed through gales of revisions and then skillfully brought *Full Speed Ahead!* into harbor.

PICTURE CREDITS

ARCTIC OCEAN

SWEDEN ◆

FINLAND ◆

DENMARK ◆

NETHERLANDS ◆

ENGLAND ◆   BELGIUM ◆

FRANCE ◆   AUSTRIA ◆

SPAIN ◆   ITALY ◆

MINORCA ◆◆   GREECE ◆

PORTUGAL ◆   MALTA ◆

Tunis, TUNISIA ●

Portsmouth, NH ●

Hastings-on-Hudson, NY ●

Chester, PA ●● New York City, NY ●

Washington, DC ●

Stony Point, TN ●   Norfolk, VA ●

Mare Island,
Vallejo, CA ●

NORTH

ATLANTIC

OCEAN

Pascagoula, MS ●

New Orleans, LA ●● Mobile Bay, AL ●

Ship Island, MS ●

CAPE VERDE
ISLANDS ●

GALÁPAGOS
ISLANDS ●

SOUTH

ATLANTIC

OCEAN

Valparaiso,
CHILE ●

SOUTH PACIFIC

OCEAN

Cape Horn, CHILE ●